Recorder Music Through the Centuries

by Franz Zeidler

WWW.MELBAY.COM

Contents

Foreword

Recorder Music through the Centuries is a compilation of three former stand-alone volumes of recorder music: *Recorder Book of Medieval and Renaissance Music, Baroque Recorder Music* and *Classic Period Recorder Music* - all written by the same author, Franz Zeidler. All of the original texts and music are included herein, mildly edited to suit current music notation standards and textual context.

Medieval and Renaissance

Medieval and Renaissance

We understand the terms *Medieval* and *Renaissance* to signify two cultural time periods ranging approximately from the year A.D. 500 to 1500 and 1500 to 1650 respectively; yet, because artistic developments take place slowly and various styles overlap, it is impossible to establish firm dates by which such periods start or end.

The Humanist philosophy or movement originated in Italy around 1350; the first Humanists coined the term "Medieval Period" to denote the span of time in antiquity during which classical values declined (circa A.D. 500) to the rebirth of those values in the Renaissance (1500 to 1650).

For our purposes in this book, it is sufficient to know that, during these early times, music was almost exclusively vocal. With time, however, instruments found their way into sacred and secular music at an increasing rate.

This segment contains examples from these two early periods that represent the general musical style from the Middle Ages to approximately the mid-17th century.

Franz Zeidler

Gregorian Chant

The Gregorian Chant is purely melodic, one-line (monophonic) music; hence its other common name—*Plainsong*. The rhythm is free and irregular, corresponding with the natural inflections of the voice. The note values in the following example, therefore, do not indicate the precise duration of the tones.

Laus Deo Patri

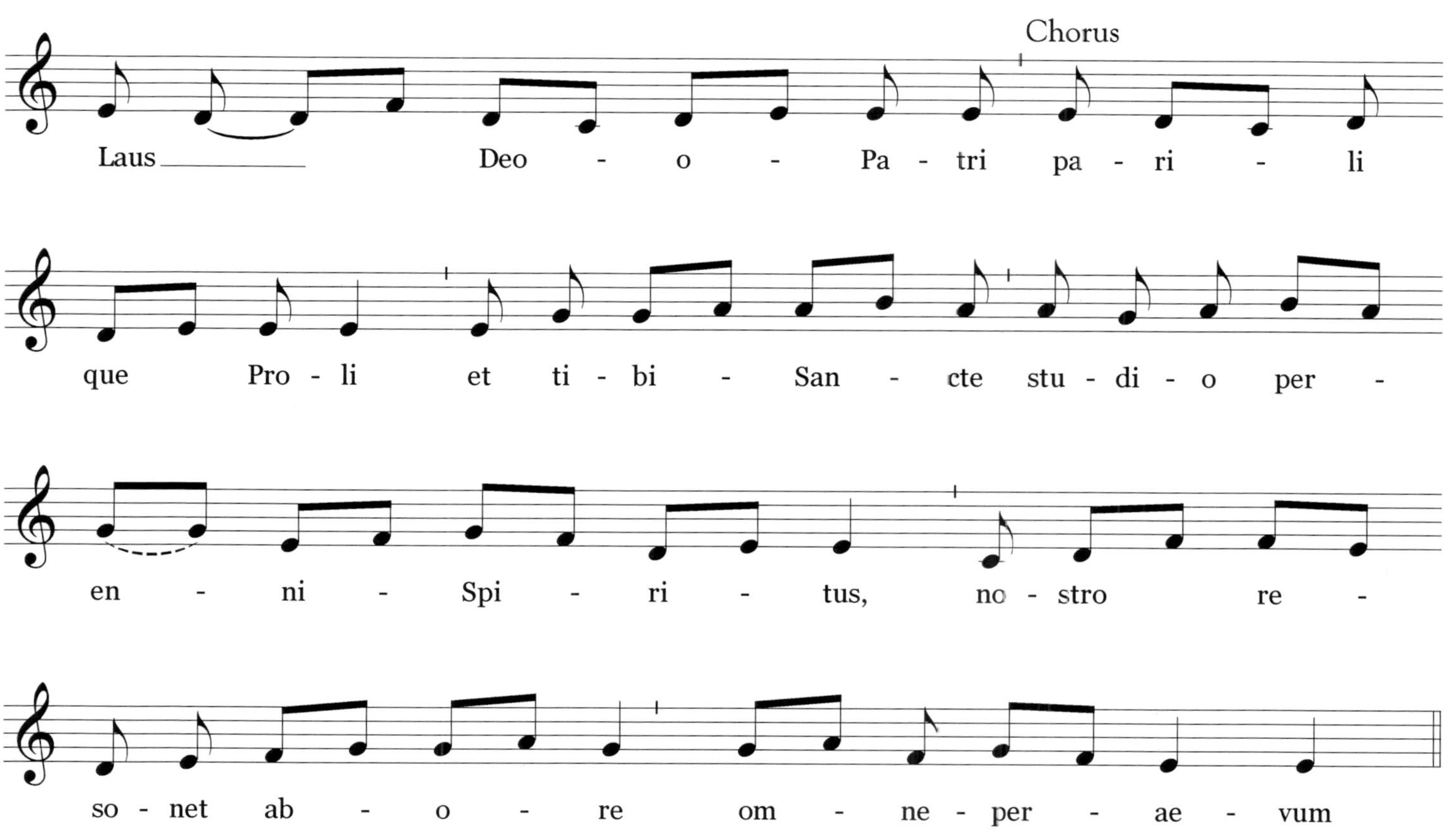

Gregorian Chant

The term Gregorian chant is applied to the solo and unison choral chants of the Roman Catholic Church. Gregorian music was composed as a monodic chant, sung in unison without any accompanying harmonic support; it has rhythmical flow and well balanced proportion of parts, but no fixed or regular structure of bars or time.

Victimae Paschali

from an 11th century Easter Mass

Troubadour Song

Secular music of the Middle Ages is represented mainly by the lyrical melodies of the *troubadours* of the twelfth and thirteenth centuries. Pictures of that period usually show the troubadour with an instrument, which very likely was used only to play brief improvised introductions, interludes and postludes.

Or la truix

12th-13th century troubadour song

Minnelied

Lyrical secular melodies, similar to those of the troubadours, occurred somewhat later in the songs of the German Minnesinger. The word *Minne* means "love." Minnelieder texts are narrative and amorous. There are also a large number of religious songs. Both types of song depict the goodness of people, the power of love and the power of God's love.

Willekommen Mayenschein

N. von Reuenthal (13th century)

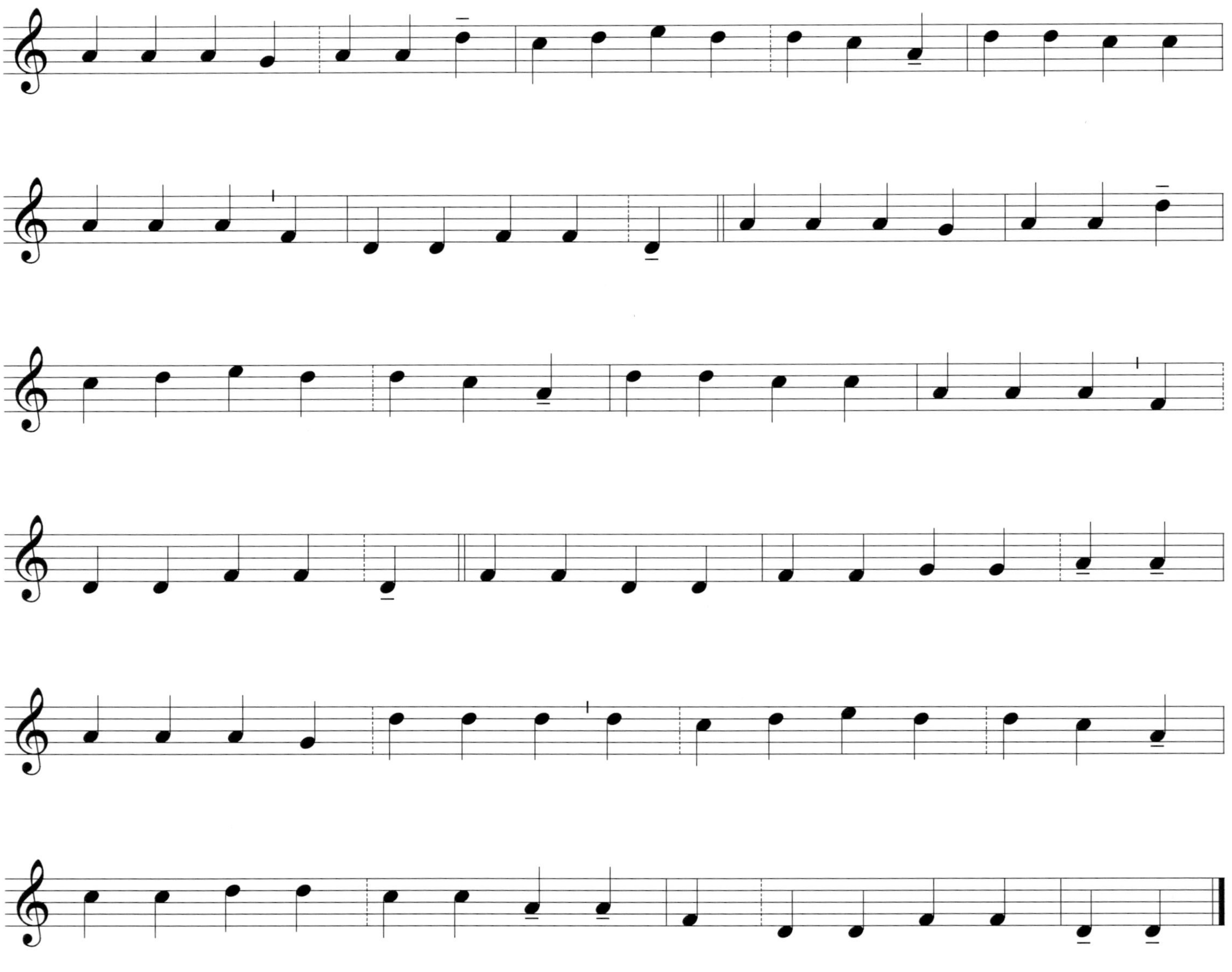

Organum

While monophonic music (music consisting of one single melodic line) was performed in those early times and while these practices were carried well into the 13th century, an important development took place in church music. Starting approximately in the 9th century, in what is today Southern Germany, Switzerland and Austria, the beginnings of polyphonic music (music consisting of more than one melodic line) were emerging. This polyphony is the root of all music in our present-day western culture.

The technique used in this new polyphony is as follows: to the existing monodic Gregorian chant, from then on called the *cantus firmus*, or later "tenor," there was added another voice, called the *organal* voice. This added voice appeared on the interval of the 4th and 5th below or above the cantus firmus. The added voice could also be doubled in the octave above or below. This type of new music was called *organum* and is the simplest and earliest type of polyphony.

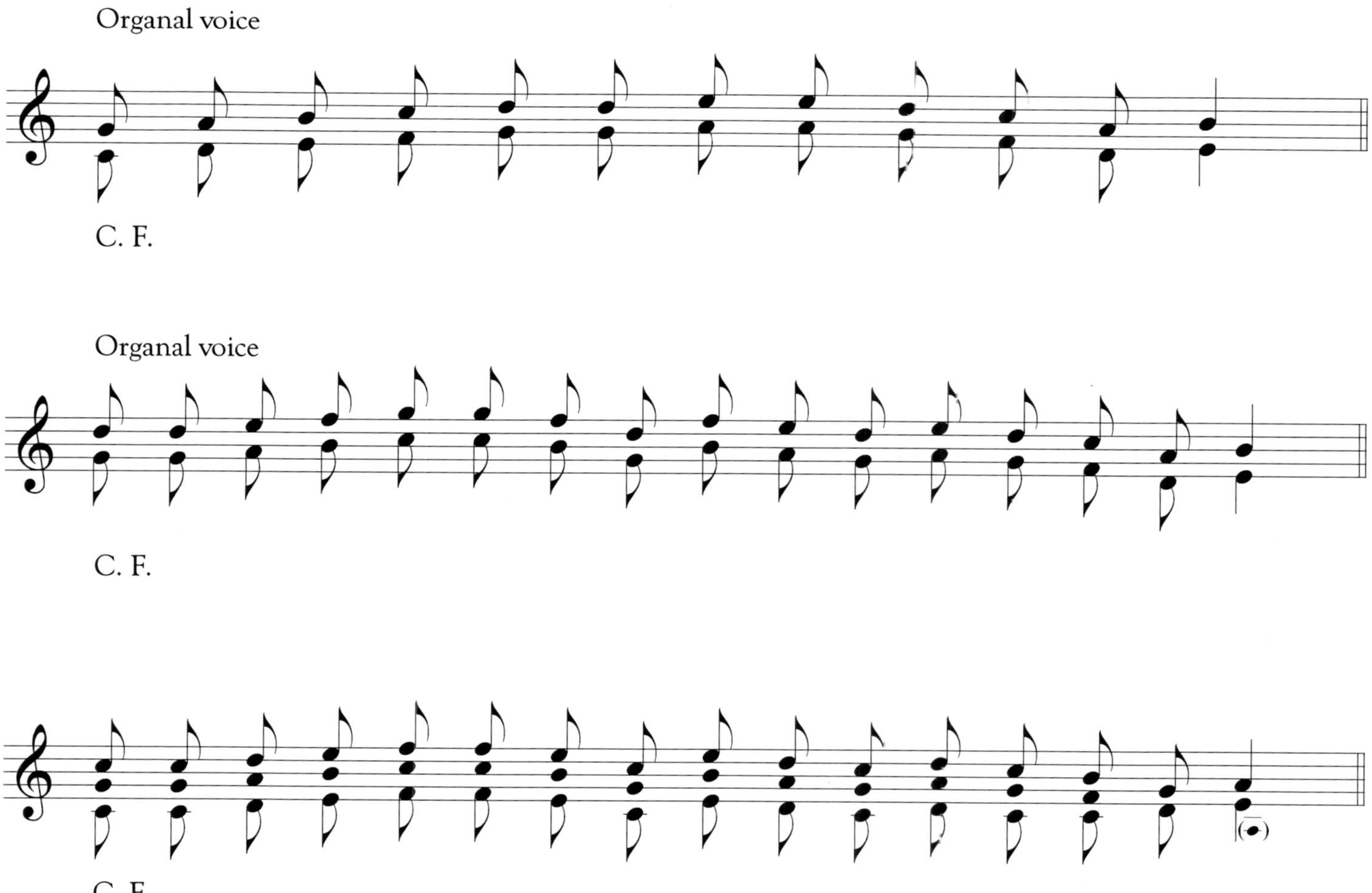

Parallel Organum

As mentioned, the earliest type of polyphonic music was called organum. The next step of development of this total paralleling of voices occured during the 9th and 10th centuries and is demonstrated in the following sample. Note that both voices start at the unison, depart, but end again in the unison sound. This is called *parallel organum.*

Rex Caeli, Domine

Parallel Organum from the 9th century

Free Organum

The next step in the development of polyphonal music occurred with the introduction of *free organum*. These compositions, also called *Tropes*, represented the most important musical progress during the 12th century. In the following sample, the trope is an insertion in the first part of the Agnus Dei. This is a two-part free organum. Rhythmically, it is similar to the earlier plainsong in its irregularity and free flow; note, however, that there is now contrary motion, different note values, and occasionally, wider intervals and voice crossings.

Free Organum

Agnus Dei

Free Organum, 12th century

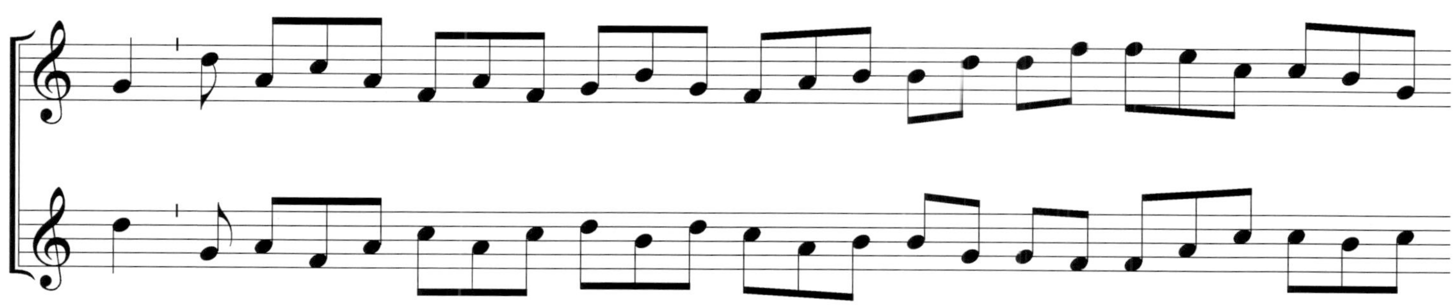

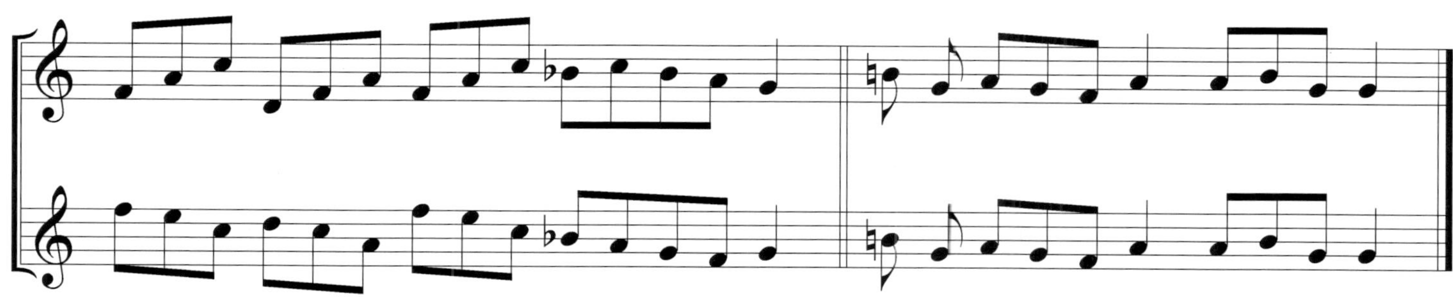

Melismatic Organum

The Abbey of St. Martial at Limoges in France was the location of an important school in the development of organum during the years from about 1100 to 1150, preceeding the more famous school of Notre Dame. In the St. Martial style, the lower voice, or tenor, uses a phrase of Gregorian chant with each note greatly prolonged, while the upper (organal) voice puts elaborate melismas in free rhythm against each tenor note. At the beginning point of phrases, the two voices form the interval of a unison, fourth, fifth or octave; between these points the tenor voice behaves in the manner of a "pedal point" against the upper voice, while the upper voice moves freely over consonant and dissonant notes at will.

Benedicamus Domino

Melismatic Organum
from the Abbey of St. Martial

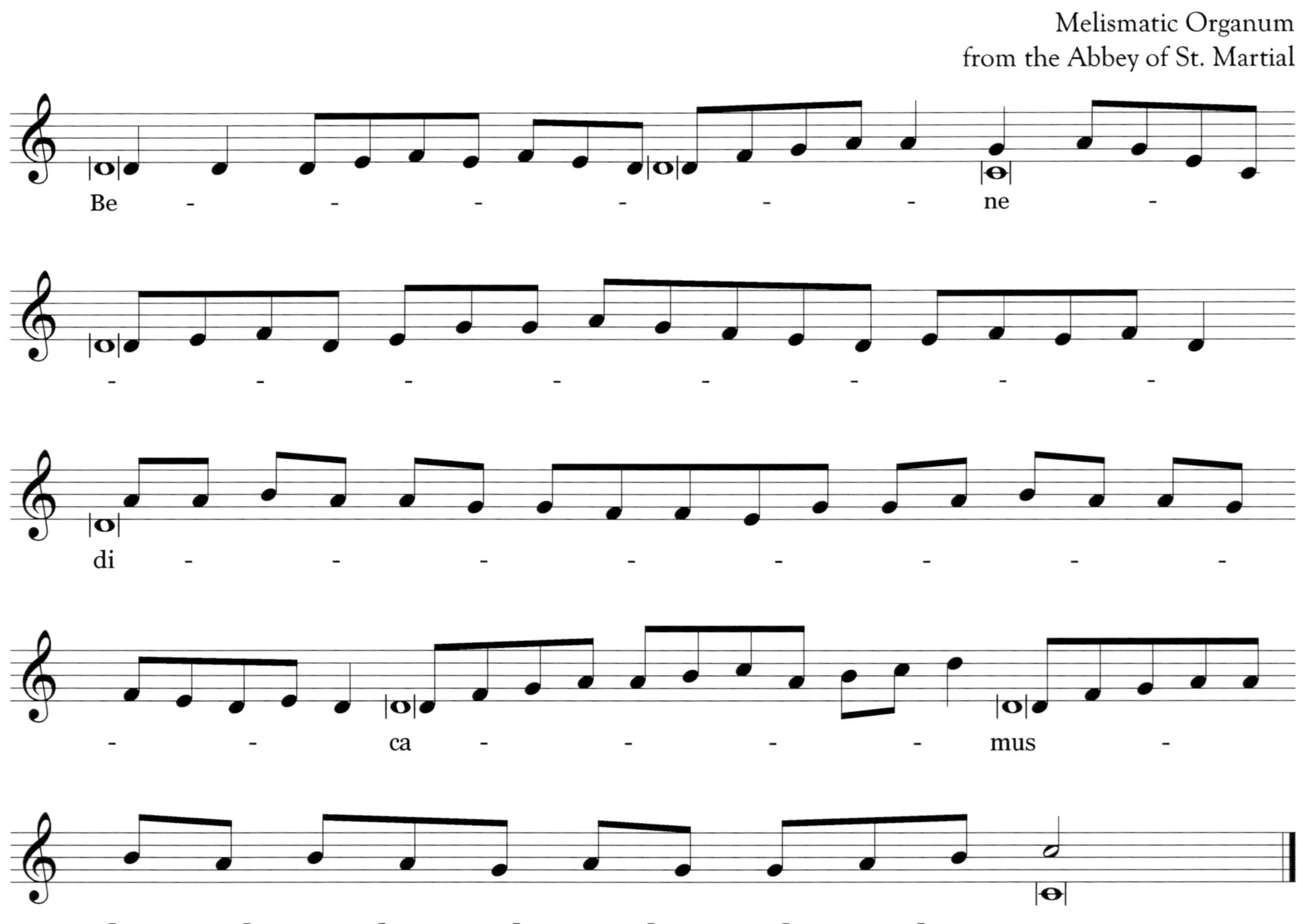

Notre Dame School Organum

Near the middle of the 12th century, the Parisian Cathedral of Notre Dame became the center of musical development. The school maintained its dominant position throughout the 13th century when the outstanding composer was Perotin. All compositions of this school are collected in the *Magnus liber organi* (The Great Book of Organa).

Alleluya (Nativitas)

Organum by Perotin

Note the increased complexity of the music picture.

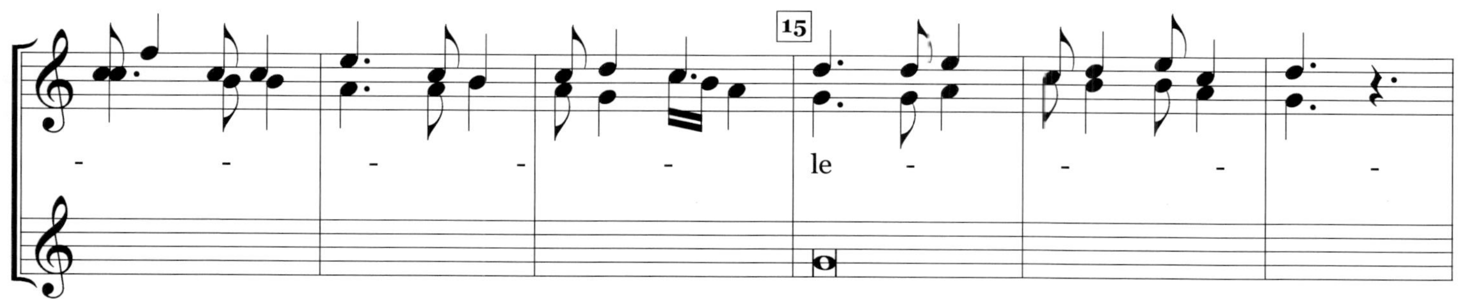

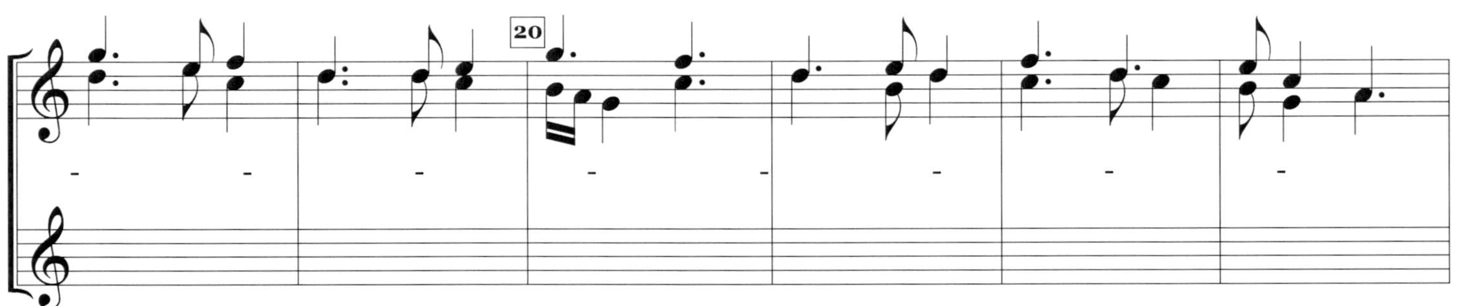
20

25

30
35
lu

40
ya

45

50

55
60

Conductus
(Secular Music)

The reason the church took the lead in musical progressive innovations is that at this time, most scholars were employed by the church. However, secular music soon had its new type of music also, even though the general structure borrowed heavily from the organum. These Latin songs, called *conductus*, were based on a "tenor," however; this tenor or *cantus firmus* was not a Gregorian chant but a free invention of the composer. Another characteristic of the conductus is that the upper voice was not as freely flowing as in the melismatic organum of free organum. The voice above the tenor is for the most part rhythmically identical with the tenor (isorhythmic), so that a note - against - note style results. The following is a sample of this type of music.

20
25
30
35

Ballata
(Ballad)

About a hundred years after the innovation of the conductus, another type of song emerges in Italy, the *Ballata*. This type became popular during the 14th century in Italy during a period that we call the "Ars Nova." Although this new music shows some French influence, a new progressive spirit is very much in evidence in this natural and spontaneous Italian style. The chief composer of this period is Francesco Landini. His style does not use the isorhythmic technique of the conductus. As far as the lower voice is concerned, it is not treated as cantus firmus but progresses in such a way that it supports the upper voice with somewhat more sustained notes, as our following example shows.

Francesco Landini

Renaissance

The music of the Renaissance period consists mainly of vocal polyphony. This type of music does not lend itself too readily to be played on the recorder. Although we are not concerned with vocal music in this book, the person interested in music should remember that people like de Machaut, Dufay, Binchois, Ockeghem, Obrecht, Josquin de Prez, Gabrieli, Orlando di Lasso, Caccini, Monteverdi, Schuetz, Frescobaldi, and Corelli to name just a few, were musical giants and their works became milestones in the history of vocal polyphony of the Renaissance. These people made major contributions to what is often referred to as the "incredible treasure of vocal polyphony of the Renaissance."

In the late Renaissance, however, the recorder as we know it became very popular for the first time in history. The following are some songs and dances that were played on the recorder as well as on other instruments.

Note also, that as the Renaissance emphasized wordly enjoyment to a higher degree than ever before, and the Medieval church had emphasized preparation for the life after the earthly life, the titles of secular music now appear in the vernacular language.

Country Jig

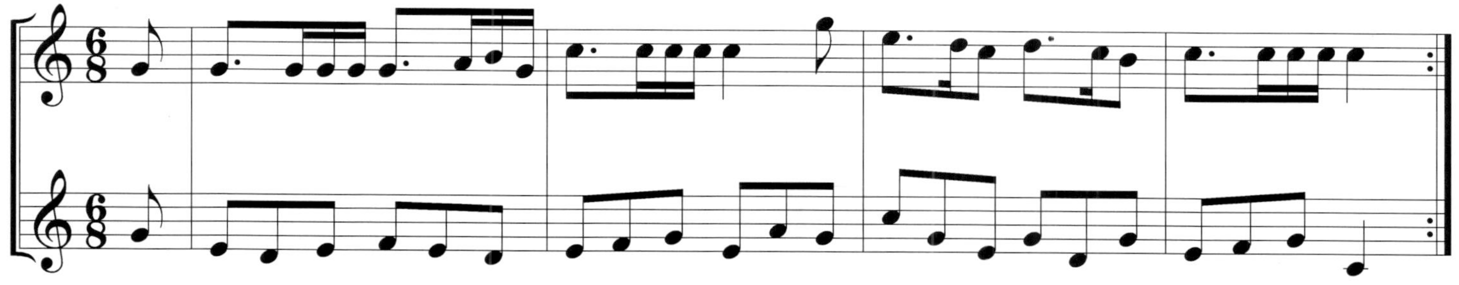

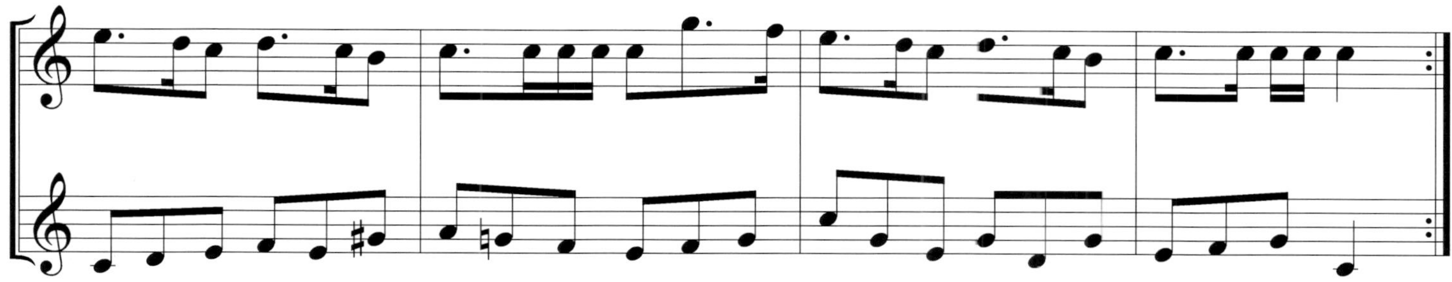

Cavalier Dance

Elbow Dance

Dutch Windmill

Little Country Dance

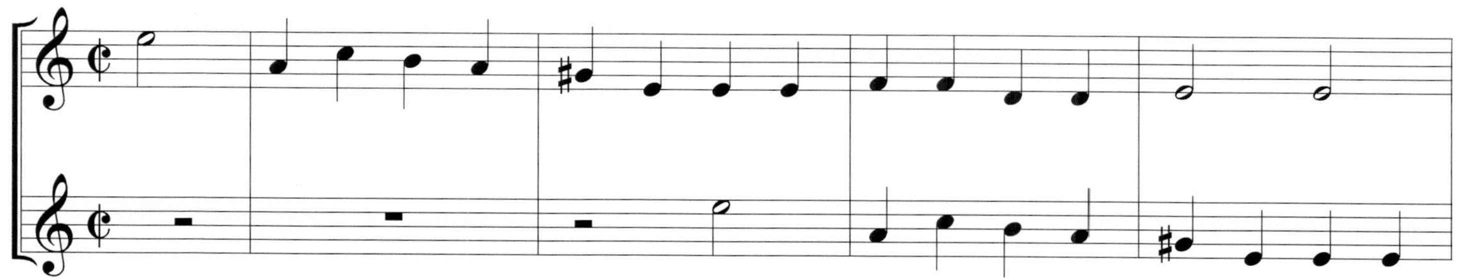

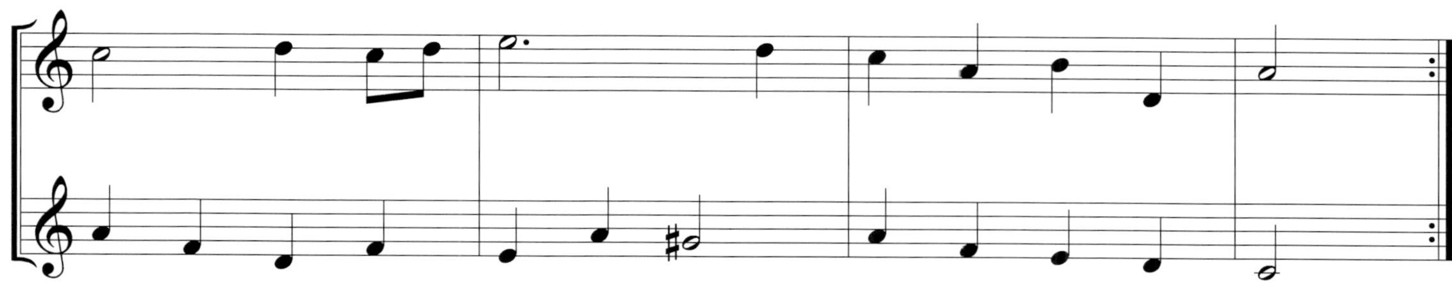

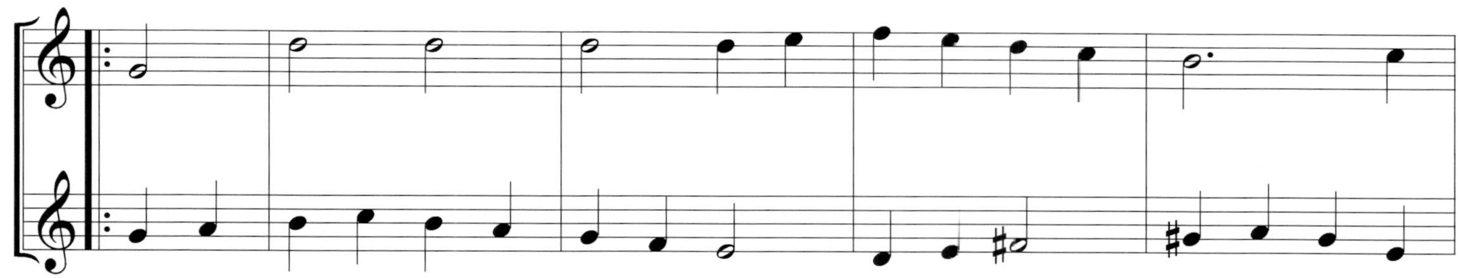

Menuet

Menuet

Baroque

Baroque

We understand the term "Baroque" to describe a period of time and a certain prevailing musical style that lasted from approximately 1650 to 1750. The best known composers of that period are Bach and Handel. Though the most typical style of that area is represented in the music for organ, harpsichord and the "Baroque Orchestra," the recorder still plays a very special role in this period.

Due to the relatively easy fingering system, simple tone production and modest price of the recorder, ordinary citizens in large numbers were able to acquire instruments and play and perform independently of others, and so became the carriers and perpetuators of music. Up to that time, the church and dukes and kings employed the musicians and composers, so music of any consequence was performed almost exclusively in their courts.

The recorder became particularly popular in England from 1500 to about 1750. During that time, a person was not considered very educated if he could not read music or play the recorder.

In the middle of the sixteenth century, recorders were built in "families" or "chests," consisting of treble, alto, tenor and bass recorders. After 1750, the German transverse, side-blown flute rapidly displaced the recorder, as the orchestra and larger ensembles required a wider range and stronger, more variable tone. In 1910, however—again in England, a very strong revitalization of recorder playing began with Arnold Dolmetch as its principal promoter; from there, the recorder's popularity spread all over Europe and North America.

Today, we find the recorder mainly used in home and school music programs but a large number of universities and colleges teach early music using the recorder. There are also several professional groups that travel and perform early music on recorders and replicas of instruments used during these early times.

Recorder music of the Baroque Period is almost exclusively secular music, so most of the examples in this section are secular in nature.

Franz Zeidler

Gavotte

N. de Chédeville

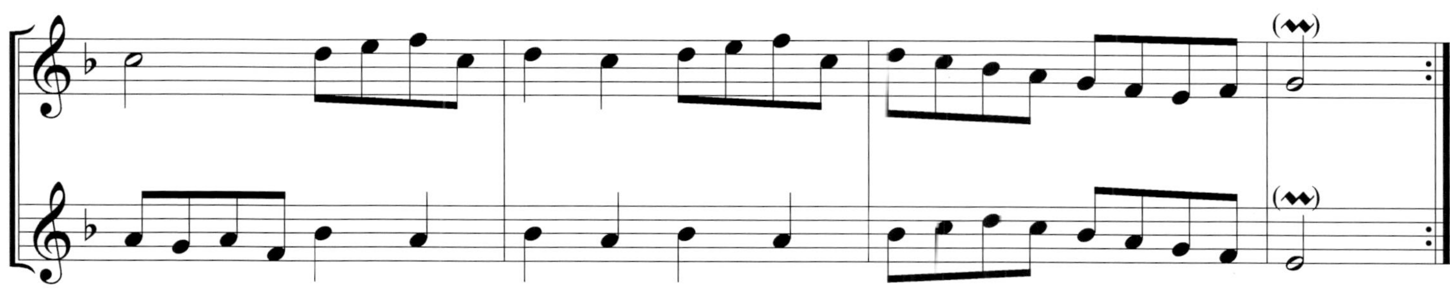

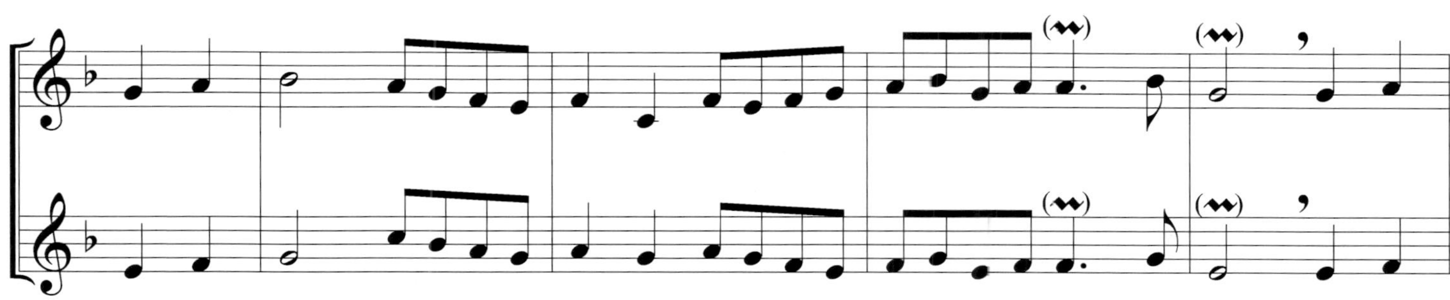

Menuet and Trio

J. Aubert

1.

2.

1.

2.

Fine

Trio

D.C. al Fine

Rigaudon

C. Baton

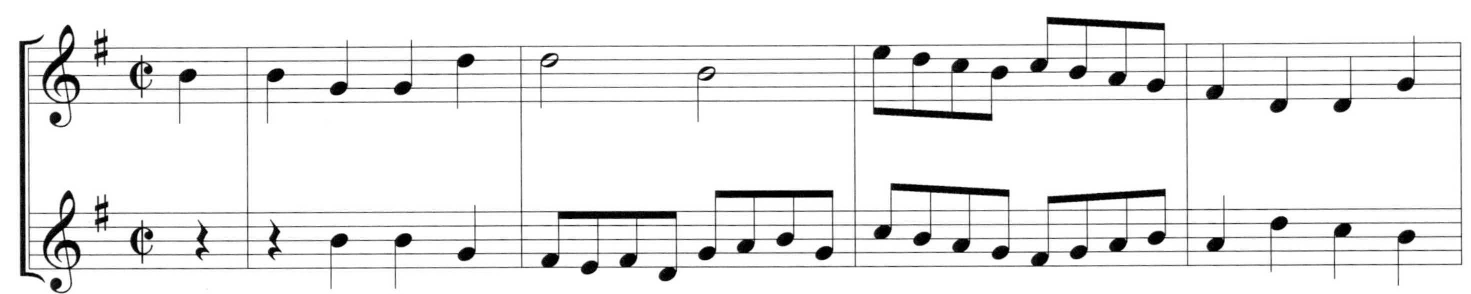

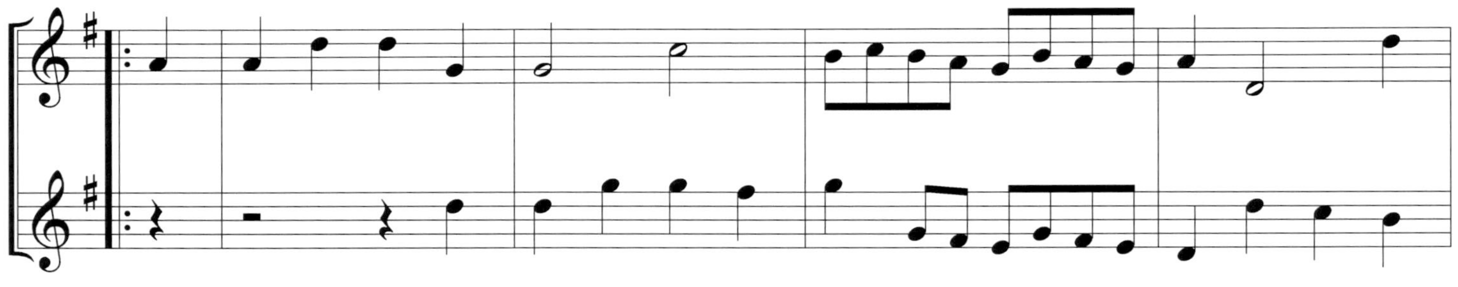

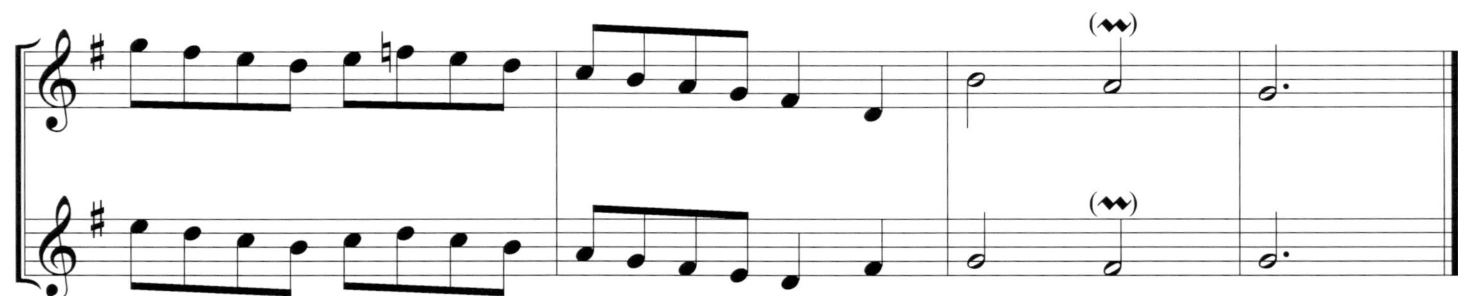

Bourrée

J. Banister

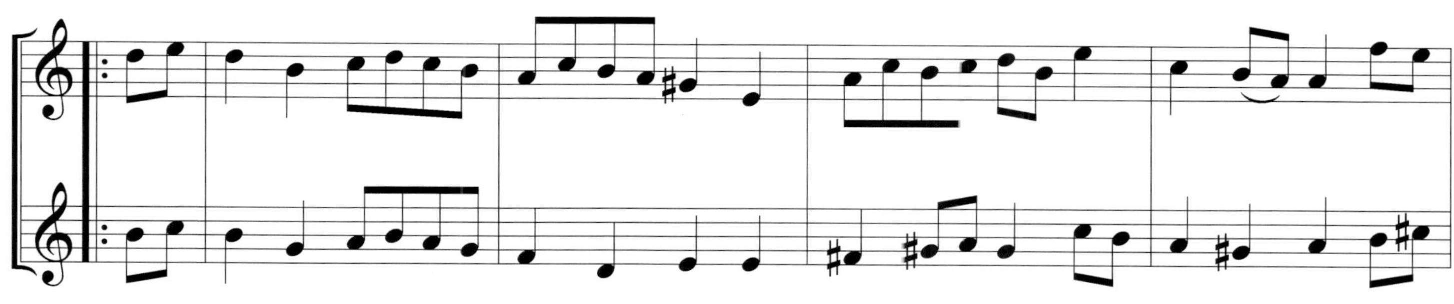

Gigue

J. Eccles

Minuet

J. Banister

Two-Part Canon

Anonymous, harmony by M. Praetorius

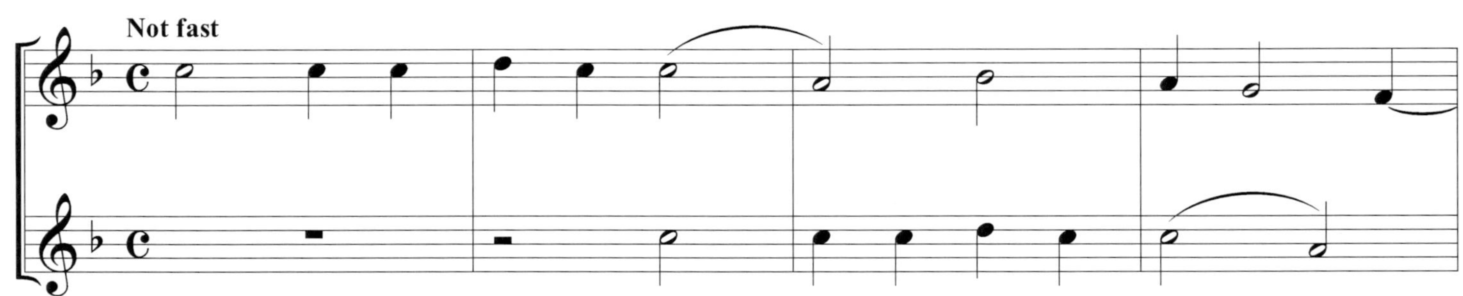

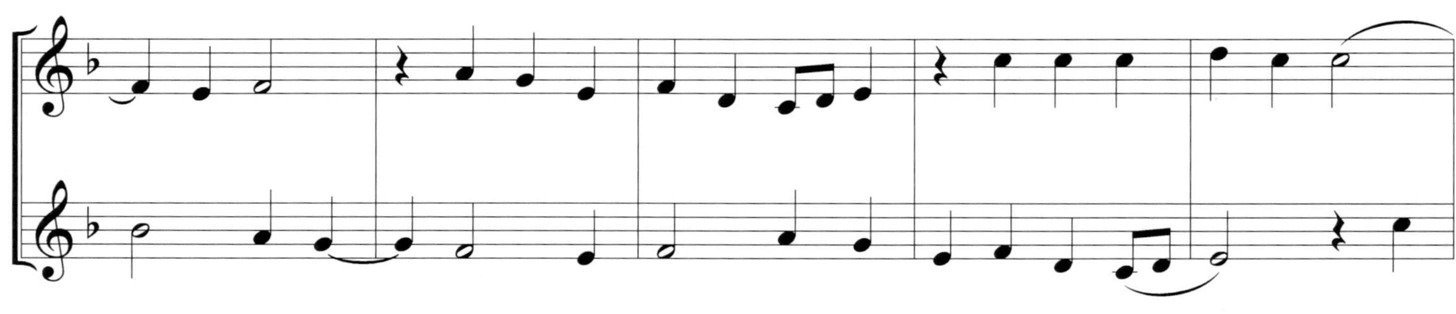

Stretto on the Lower Second

F. Geibel

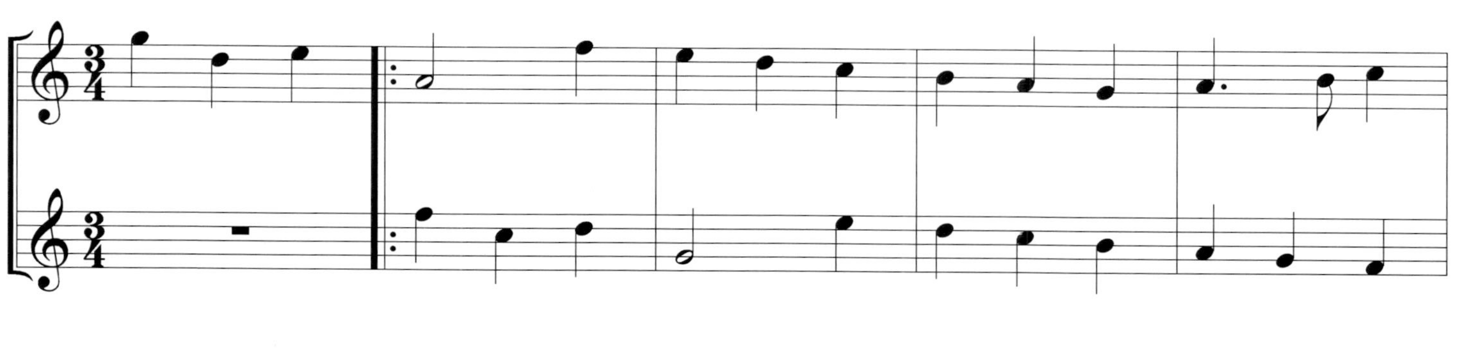

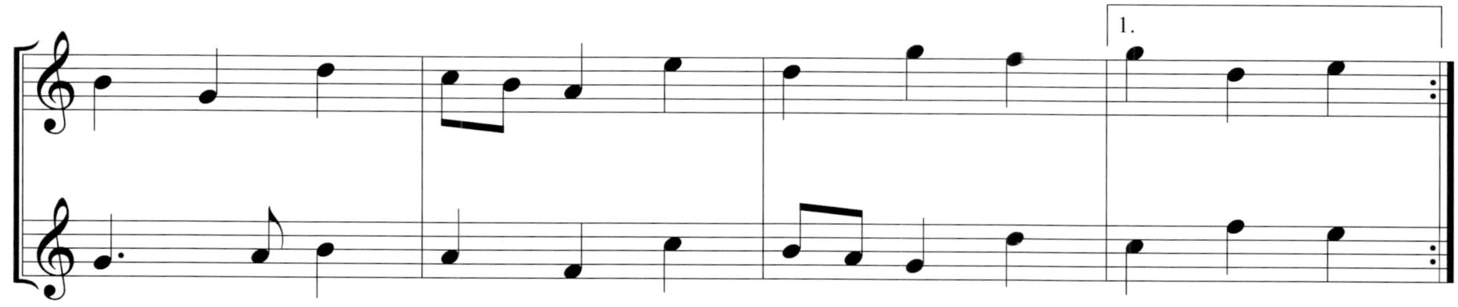

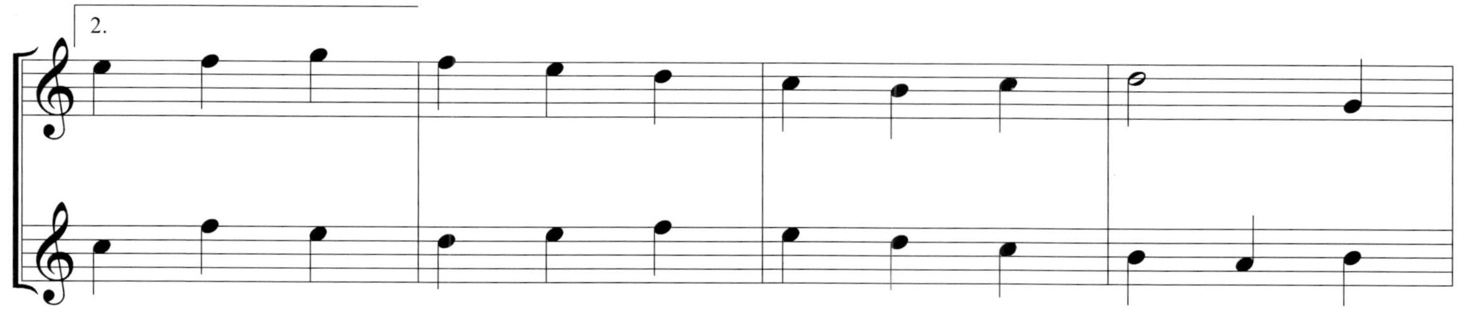

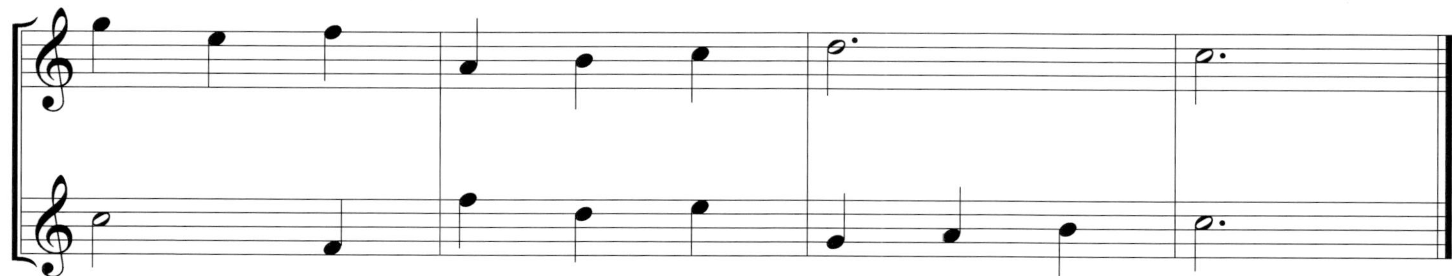

Fanfare

A. de Fesch

tr

Gavotte

R. Dettbach

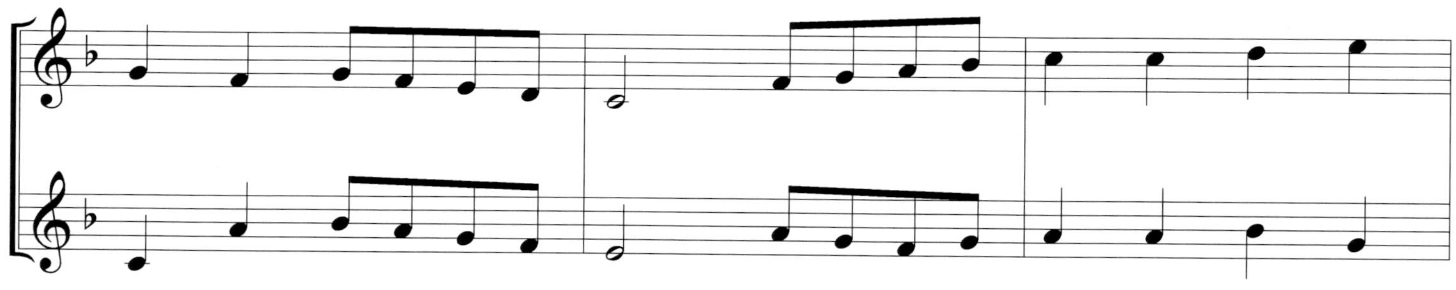

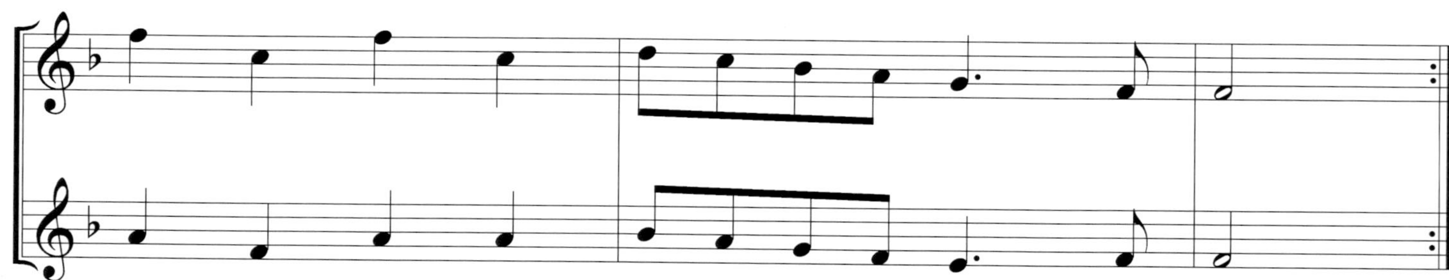

Minuet

From an 18th-century book of recorder music, composer unknown

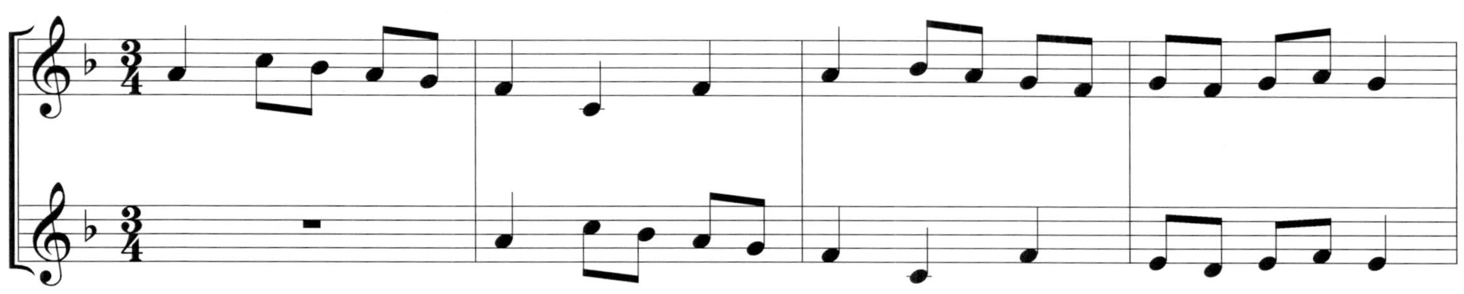

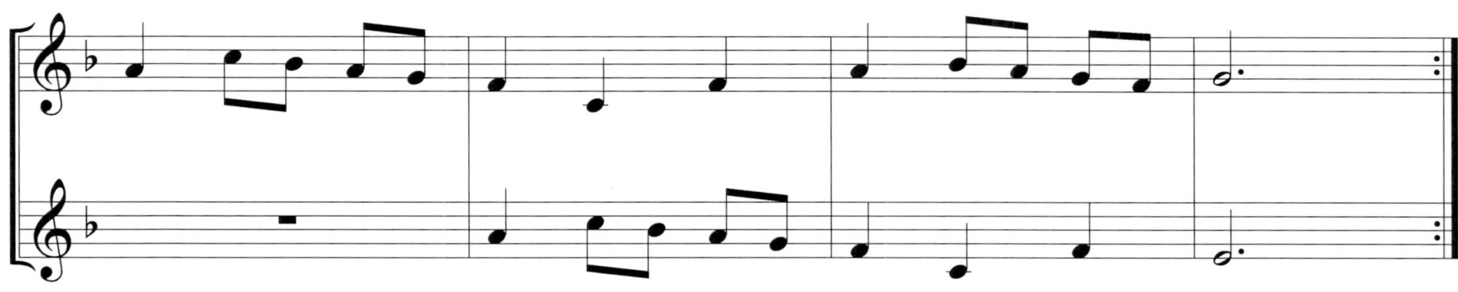

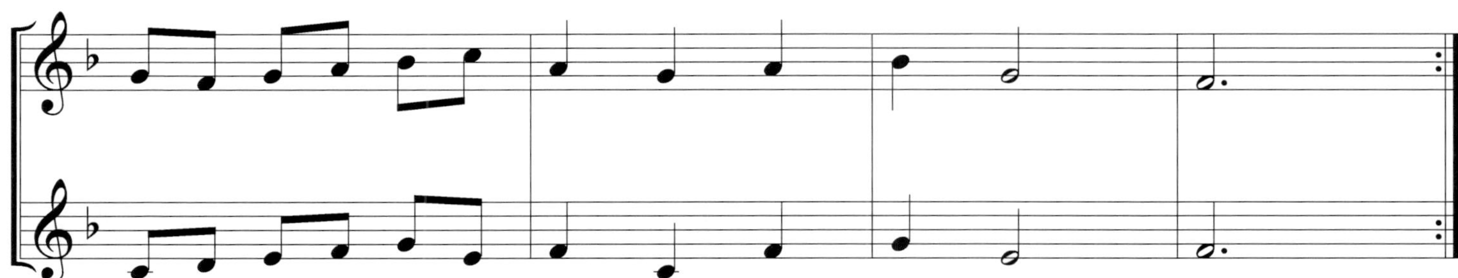

Little Echo Song

W. H. Pachelbel

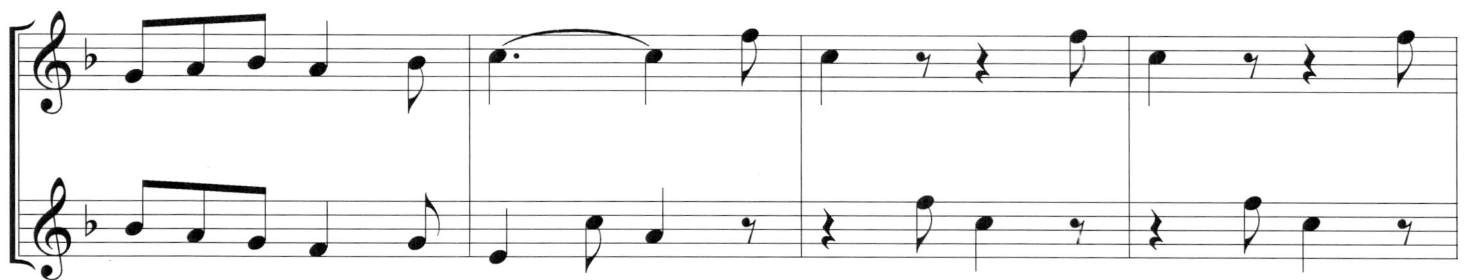

The following composition, *Canon* by Johann Pachelbel, is a very rewarding work and the recorder student should make an effort to perfect this piece. Though it is somewhat more demanding, it doesn't present the technical difficulties that one might expect in four-part music, but it does require unwavering ensemble playing skills. To look, listen and adjust one's playing to conform and contribute to producing the total musical effect that is intended with this music is, in itself, an invaluable exercise and discipline.

The Immortal Canon
Pachelbel's Canon

Johann Pachelbel

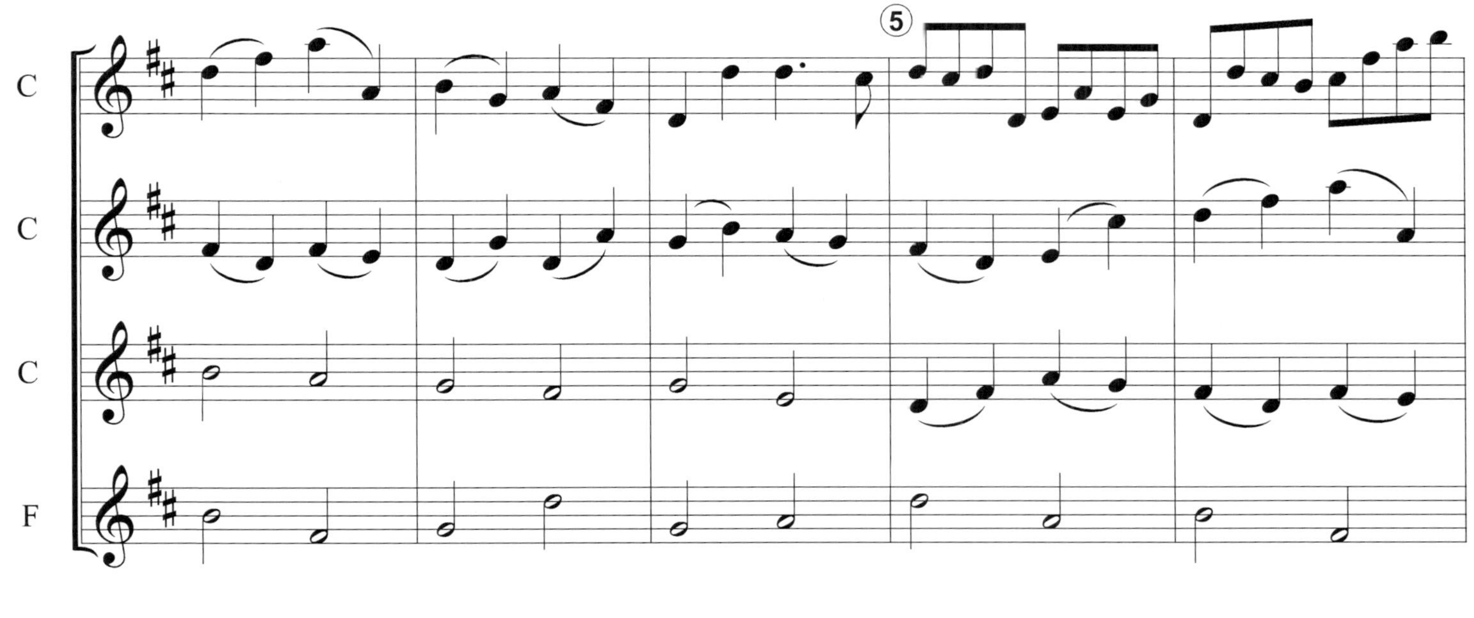
C
C
C
F
5

C
C
C
F
6

C
C
C
F
7
Original
Original
notes

8
C
C
C
F
f
f
f
f
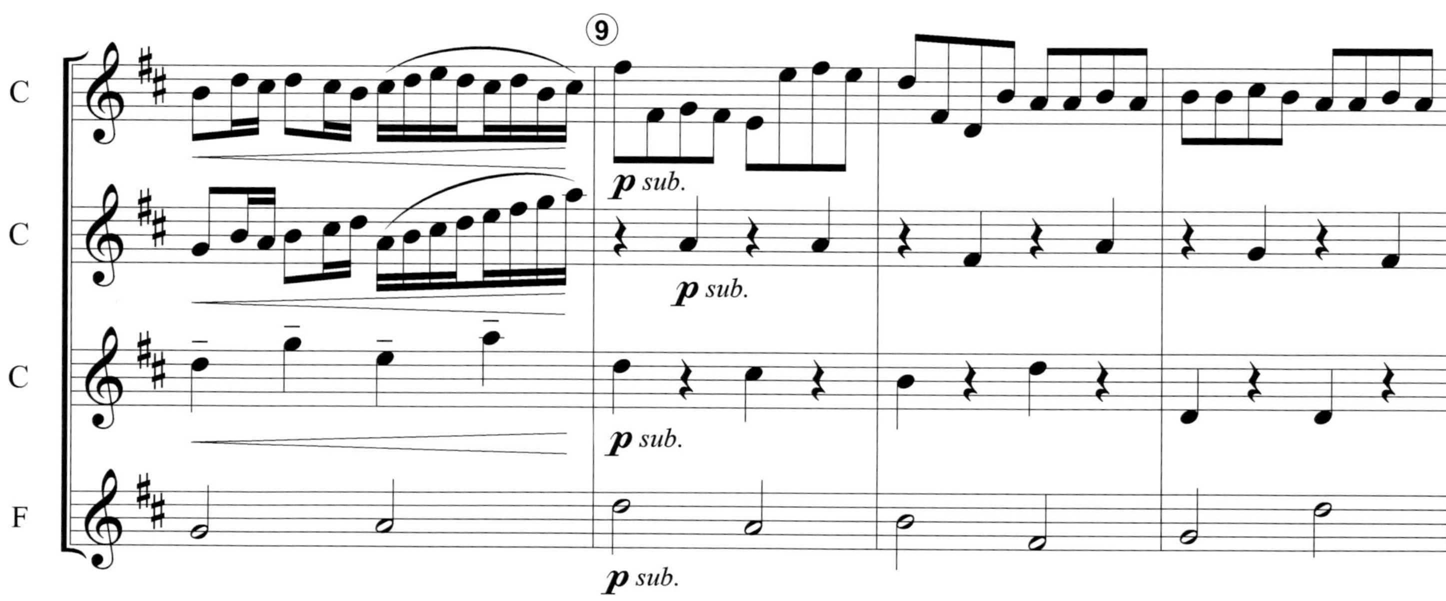
9
C
C
C
F
p sub.
p sub.
p sub.
p sub.

10
C
C
C
F

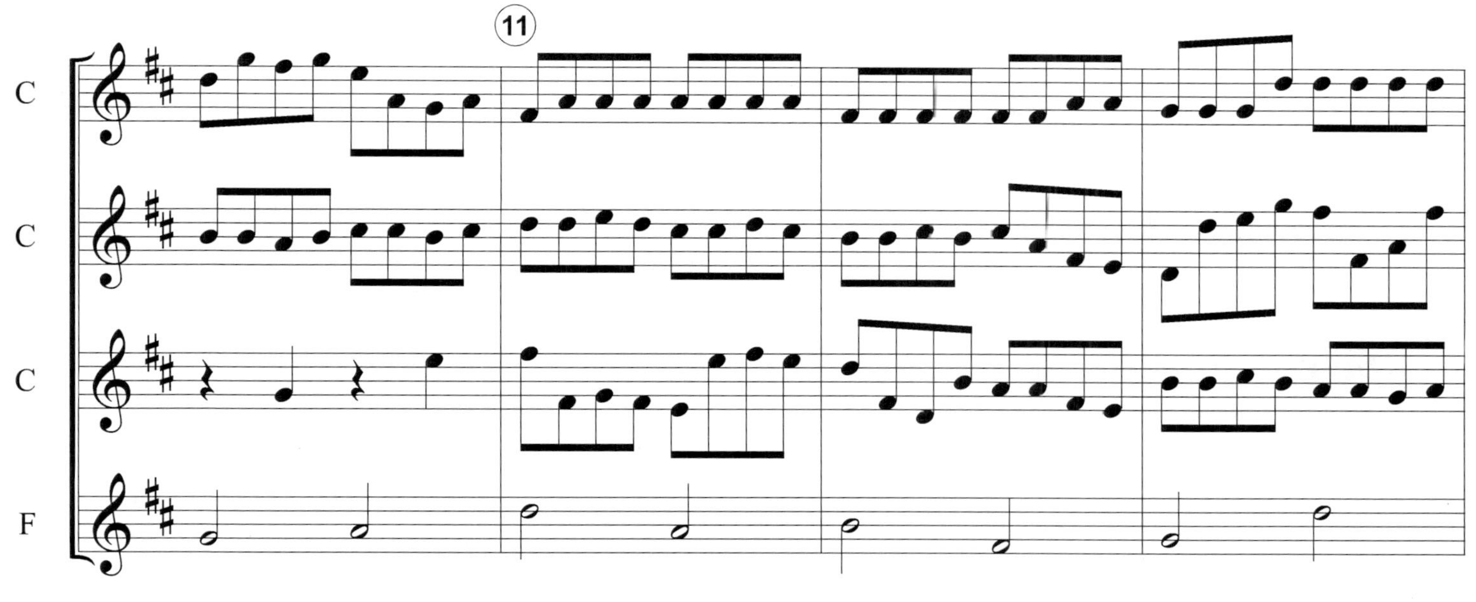
11
C
C
C
F

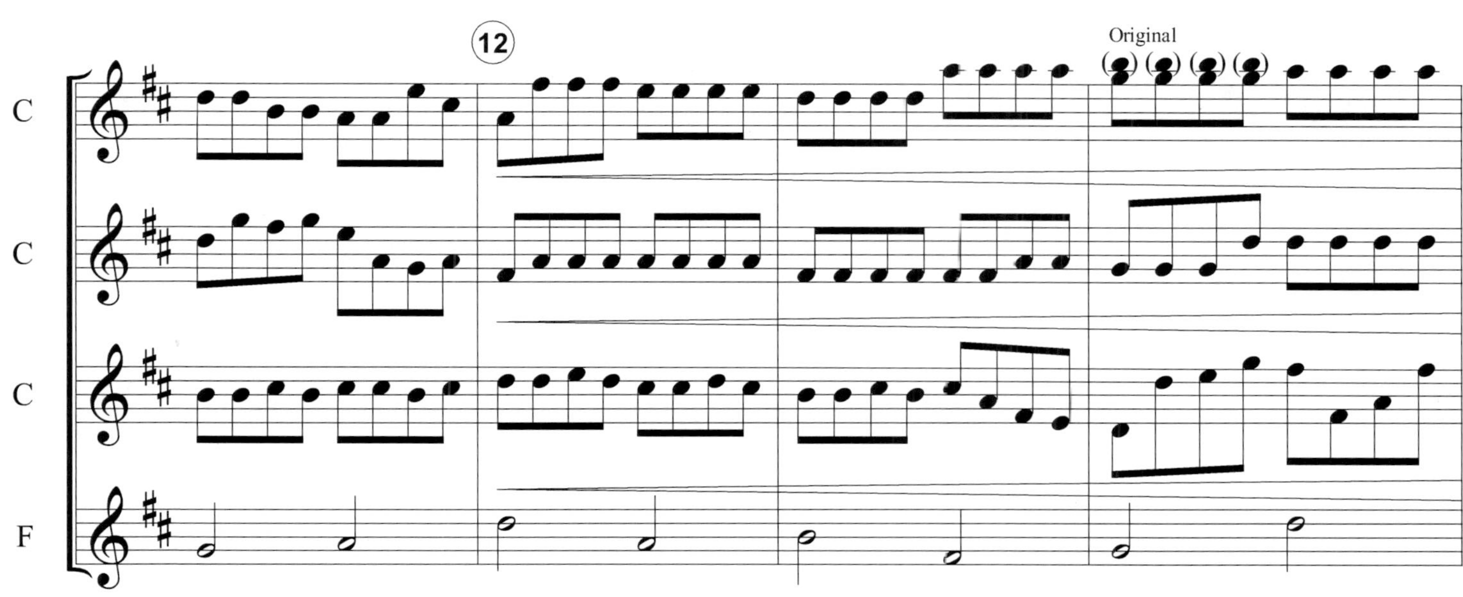
12
Original
C
C
C
F

Original notes
13
Original
C
C
C
F
mf
mf
mf
mf

14

C

Original notes

f broad

C

f broad

C

f broad

F

f broad

Caprice

From an18th century book of recorder music, composer unknown

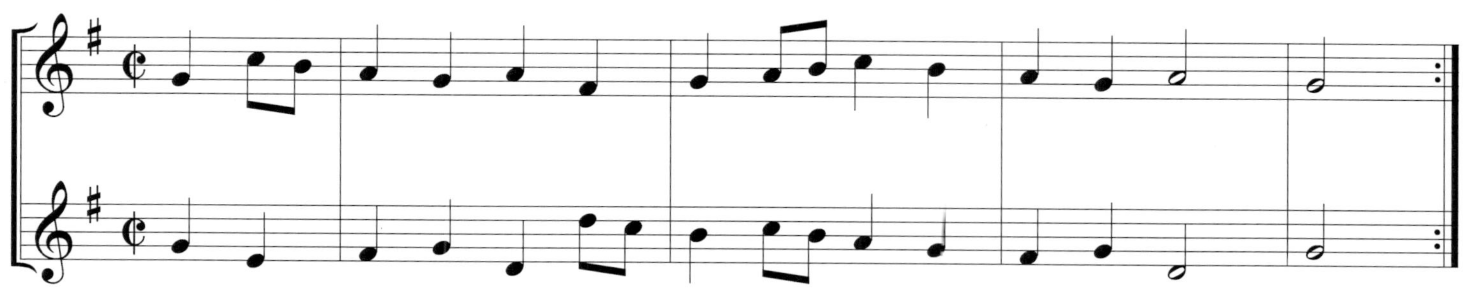

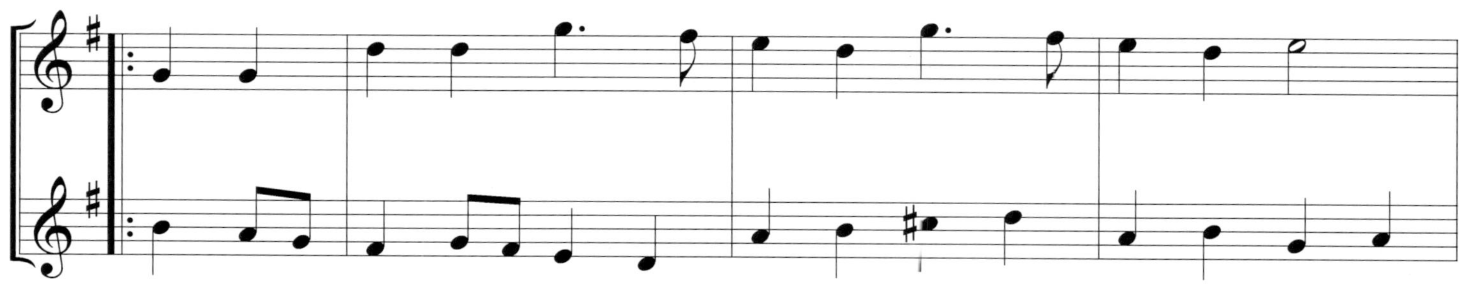

Classical Period

Classical Period

The term "classicism" is used freely in music to include the period in which instrumental and vocal forms broke away from the polyphonic style and from the influence of church music.

Eighteenth-century Vienna is considered the background of the musical "Classical Era" in which the sonata was the dominating form and of which Mozart and Beethoven are the most famous exponents. The following explanation, however, might help the student to understand the full meaning of the word classic.

The term "classic" is derived from the Latin classicus. During the time of the Roman Empire a person labeled 'classicus' was thought of as belonging to the highest tax-paying group. Tax assessment in the Roman Empire was formulated according to an individual's wealth and position; a person being called a 'classicus' consequently deemed to be materially and intellectually outstanding.

Later, there appears in Roman writings the term *scriptor classicus;* this title classified a person as an outstanding writer, one of the first ranks.

During the 19th century, this definition was expanded and applied to the highest levels of achievement in the arts, literature and education as well as to areas of general culture which met the standards of the absolute perfection. Through this extension, the term classic or classical became the name of a certain era in the history of music that is considered to be the culmination of a development, the concept of which became the measure to determine the maximum standard of performance as the ideal model and norm.

While this culmination point in the history of music occurred approximately between 1750 and 1820, a "classic" achievement in any form of art is not dependent on location or chronological distances, but solely on the quality and actual appearance of what is being judged.

The flexibility and applicability of the word classic is probably well demonstrated when one speaks of Palestrina being the "Classicist of Church Music" or the music of The Dave Brubeck Quartet being lauded as "classic jazz." To qualify as "classic" is equal to having reached the highest form of achievement in your field.

Classical music, as well as any other achievement in its classic form, is characterized by the following features: harmonious completion of the subject, and limiting of the elements of intellect and emotion-spirit and nature- to equal parts in perfect balance. The "classic" art desires to achieve in a mature creation the typical type that reflects a moral code of ethics based on order, noble greatness and clarity, all by the acceptance of a rational and sensible polarity.

Franz Zeidler

The Alphabet

A humorous intonation of the alphabet.

W. A. Mozart

Menuet in C

L. V. Beethoven

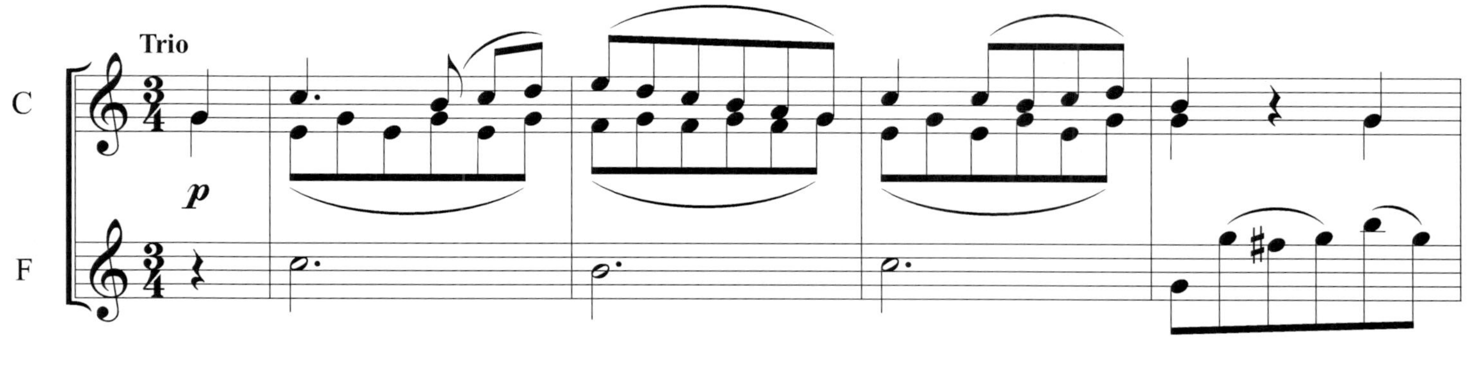
Trio
C
F
p
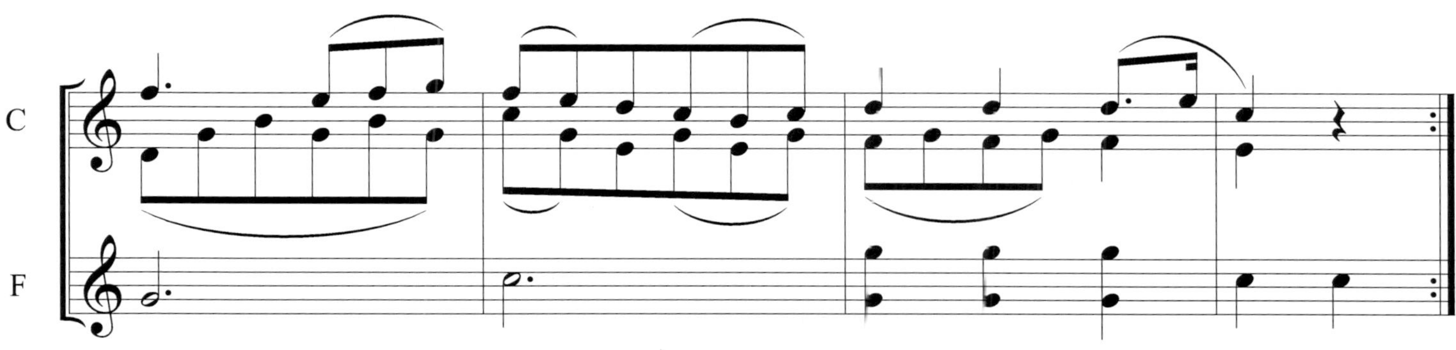
C
F
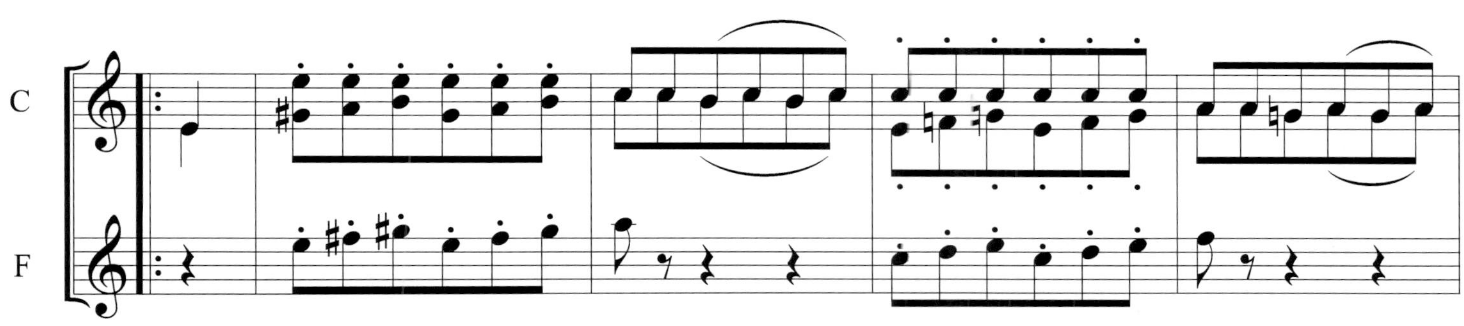
C
F
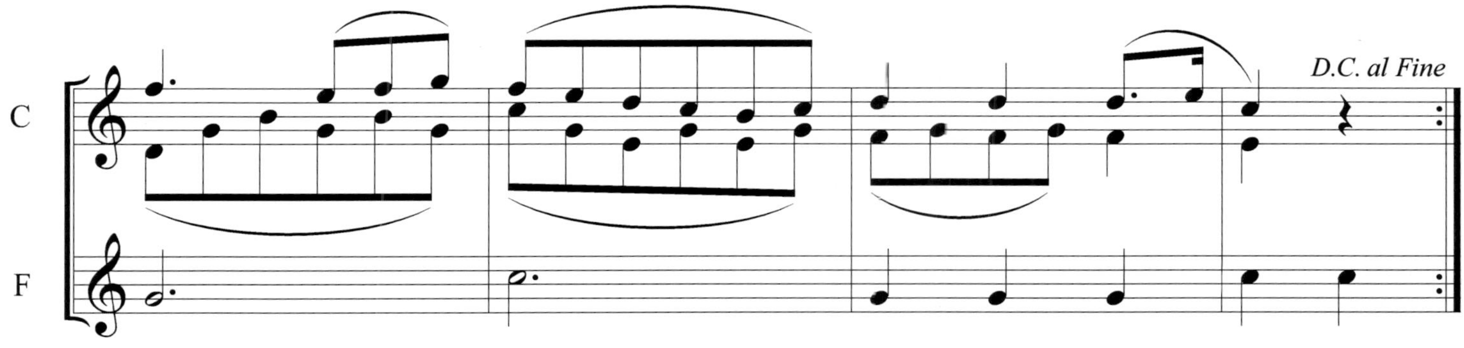
D.C. al Fine
C
F

Sonatina in G

This Sonatina consists of two movements, the "Allegro" and the "Romance."

This work will also be very pleasant if only the melody is played, without the harmony parts in the second line.

L. V. Beethoven

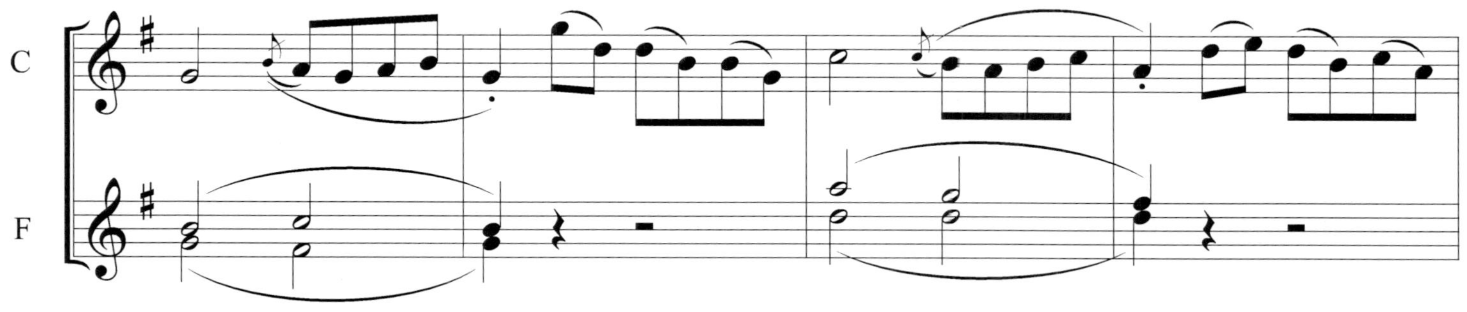
C
F

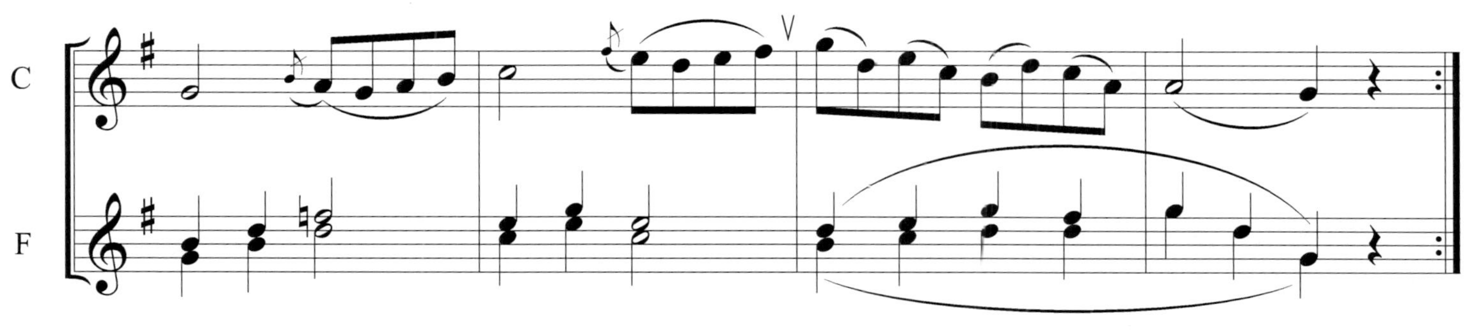
C
F

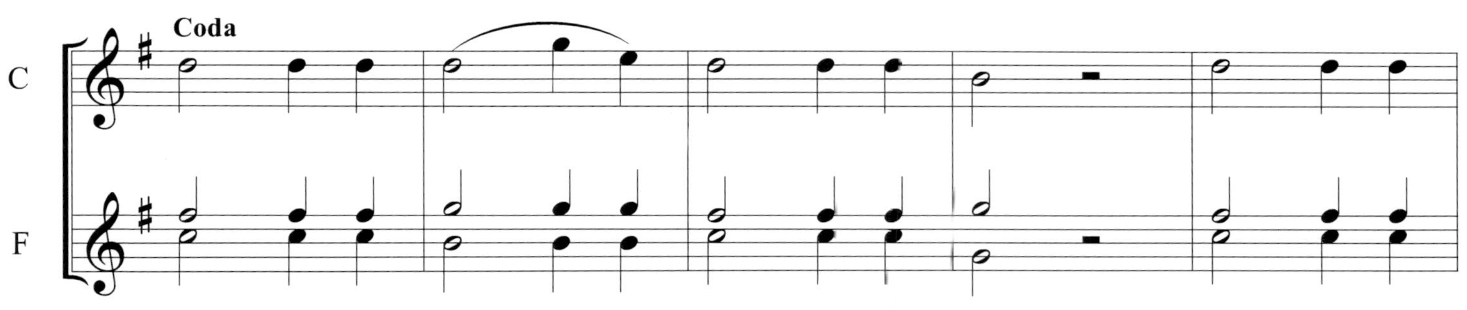
Coda
C
F

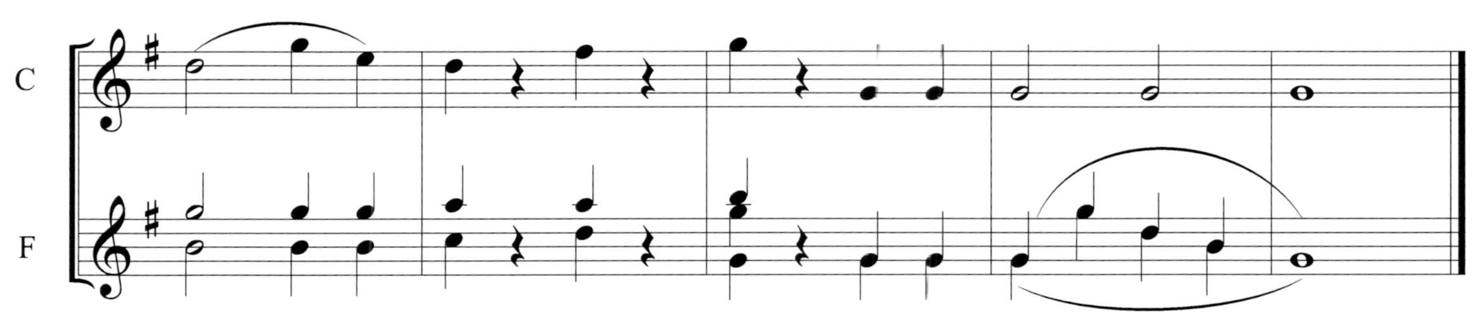
C
F

Romanze

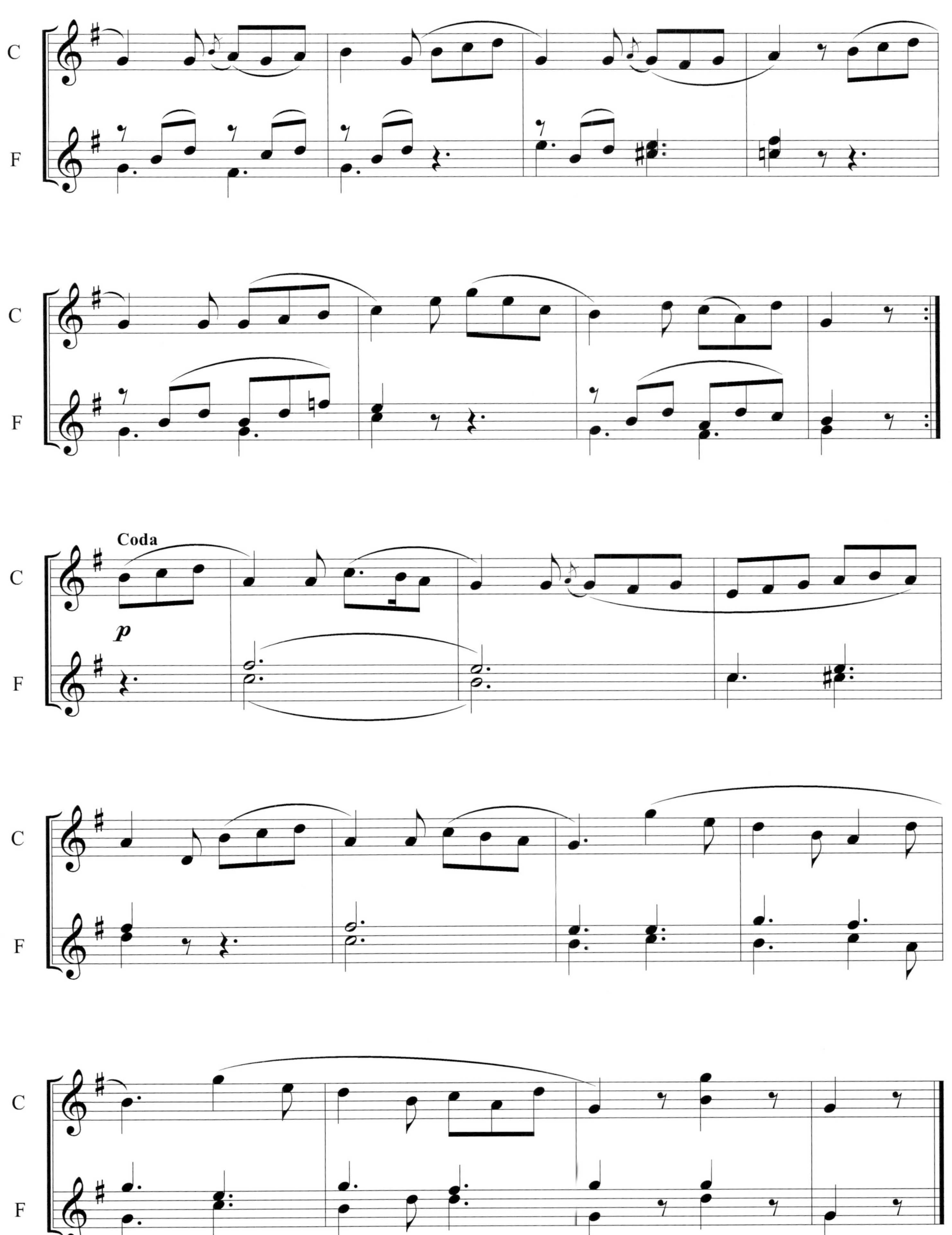
C
F
Coda
p

Little Fanfare

Austrian, composer unknown

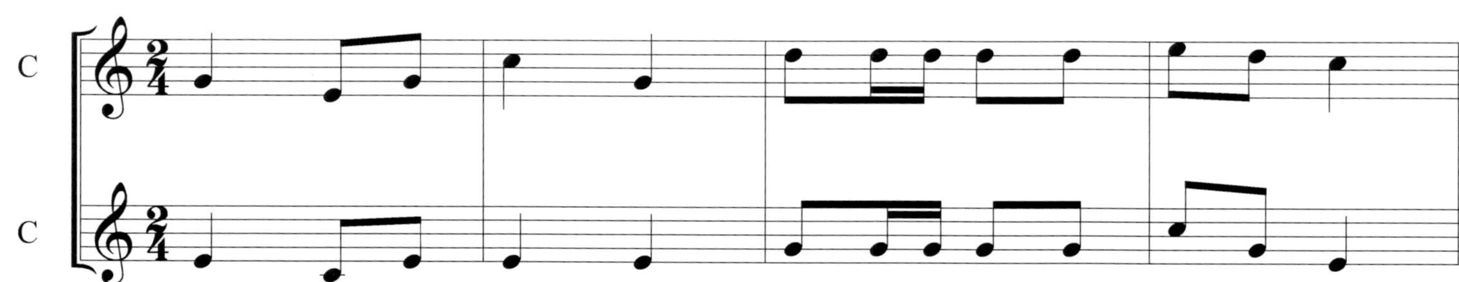

Menuet

Leopold Mozart, the father of the famous Wolfgang Amadeus Mozart, was actually not a composer. However, he wrote a fair number of shorter pieces that he used as teaching material with his young students. This Menuet is one of those pieces.

Leopold Mozart

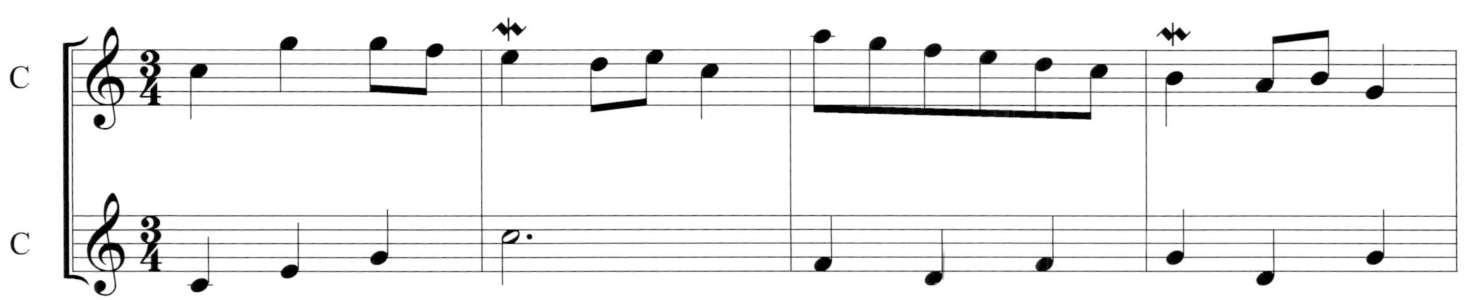

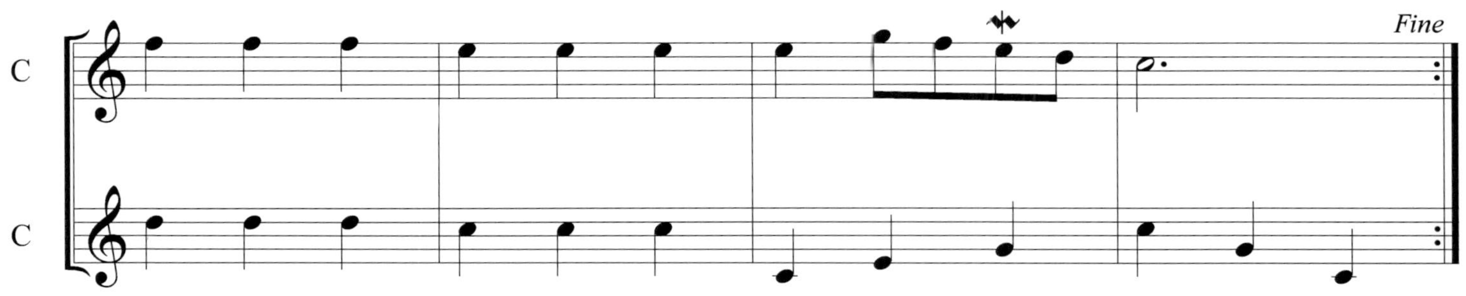

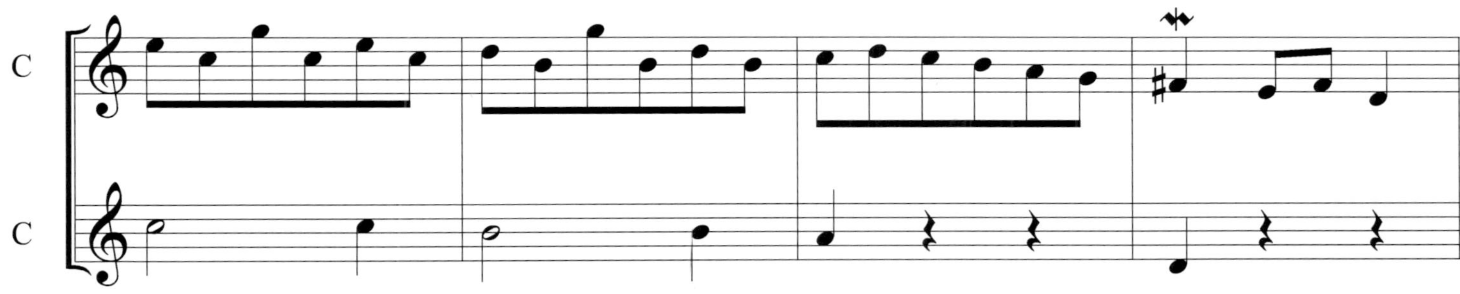

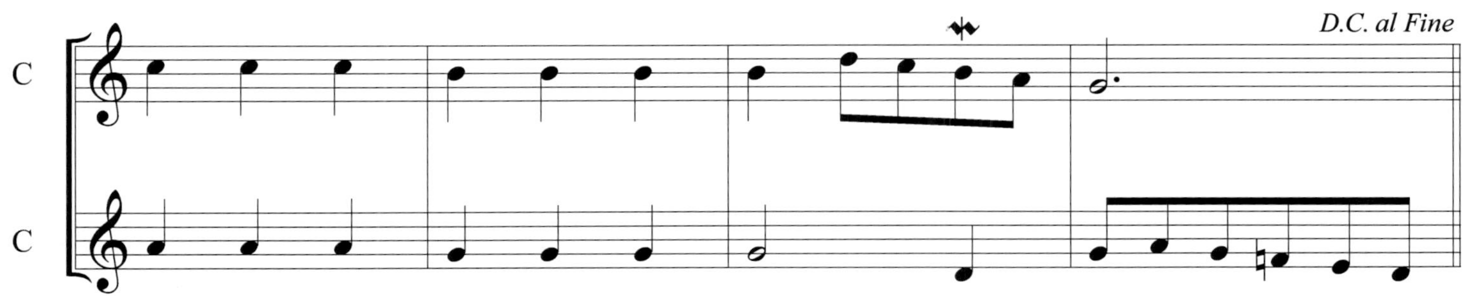

Menuet

W. A. Mozart

Little Dance

E. Steiner

Austrian March

This is another piece that Leopold Mozart composed for his students.

Leopold Mozart

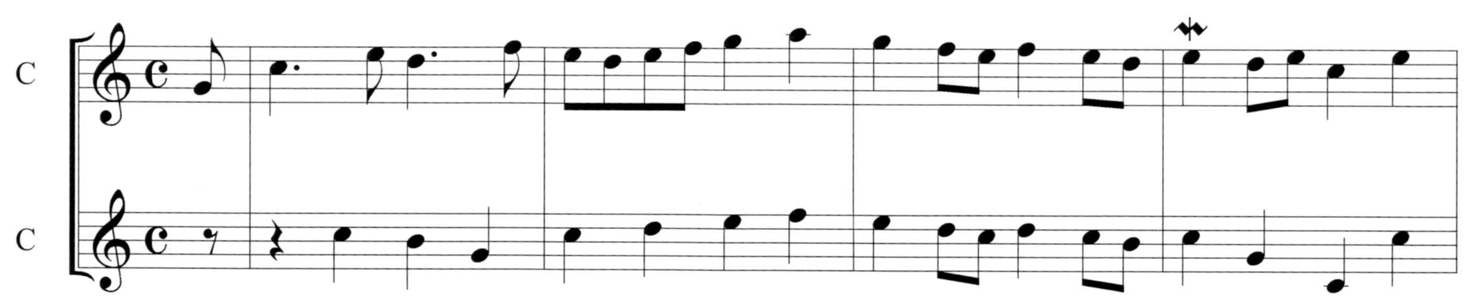

C
C
3
3
3
3
3
3
3

Alpine Dance

Folk Dance from Bavaria

Composer unknown

Themes from Classical Symphonies

Symphony No. 1 in C Major

2nd Movement

L. V. Beethoven

Symphony No. 1
3rd Movement, Trio

L. V. Beethoven

Symphony No. 1
4th Movement

Symphony No. 2 in D Major
2nd Movement

L. V. Beethoven

Symphony No. 9 in D Major

Main Theme, Last Movement (Choral Section)

L. V. Beethoven

Symphony No. 3 in E-flat Major
Main Theme, First Movement

W. A. Mozart

This page is left blank to avoid an awkward page turn.

Symphony No. 3 in E-flat Major
Third Movement, Menuetto

L. V. Beethoven

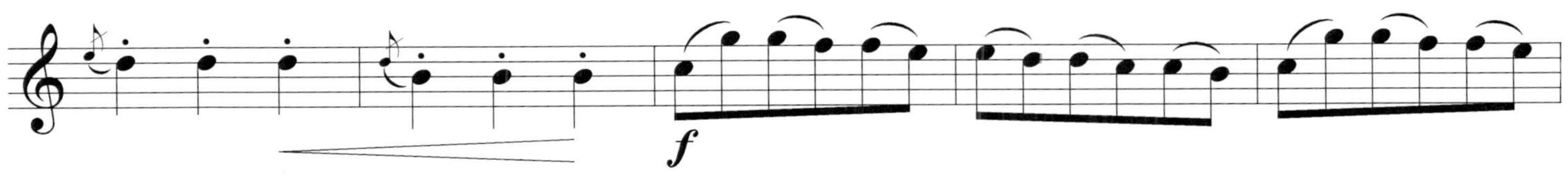
f

Fine
Trio
mf
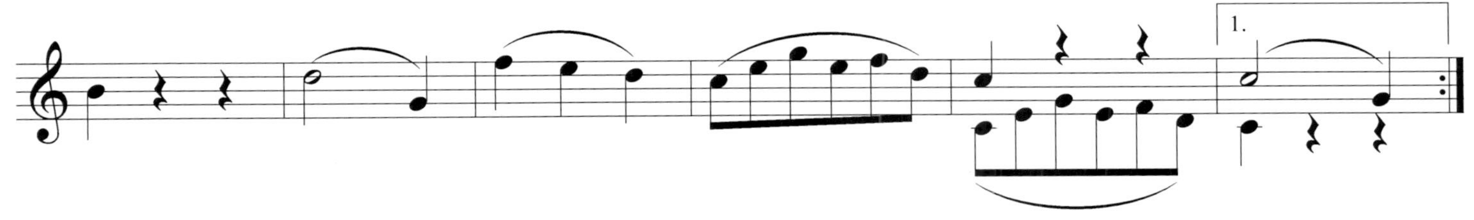
1.

2.
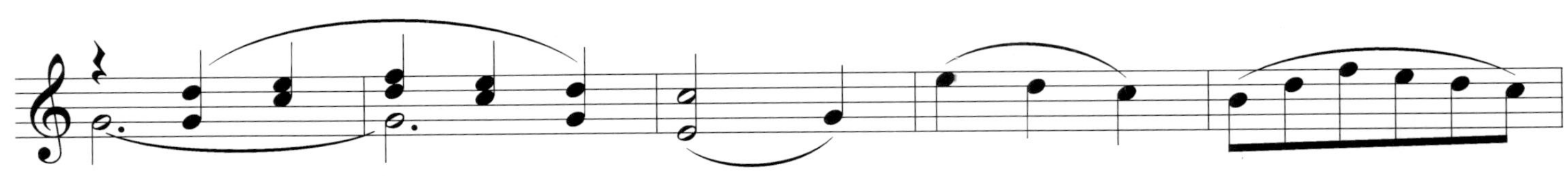

D.C. al Fine

Jupiter Symphony
Exposition, 1st Movement

W. A. Mozart

Jupiter Symphony
Principal Theme, 3rd Movement

W. A. Mozart

Surprise Symphony
Theme of 2nd Movement

Military Symphony
Main Theme of 2nd Movement

J. Haydn

Not fast

C

p

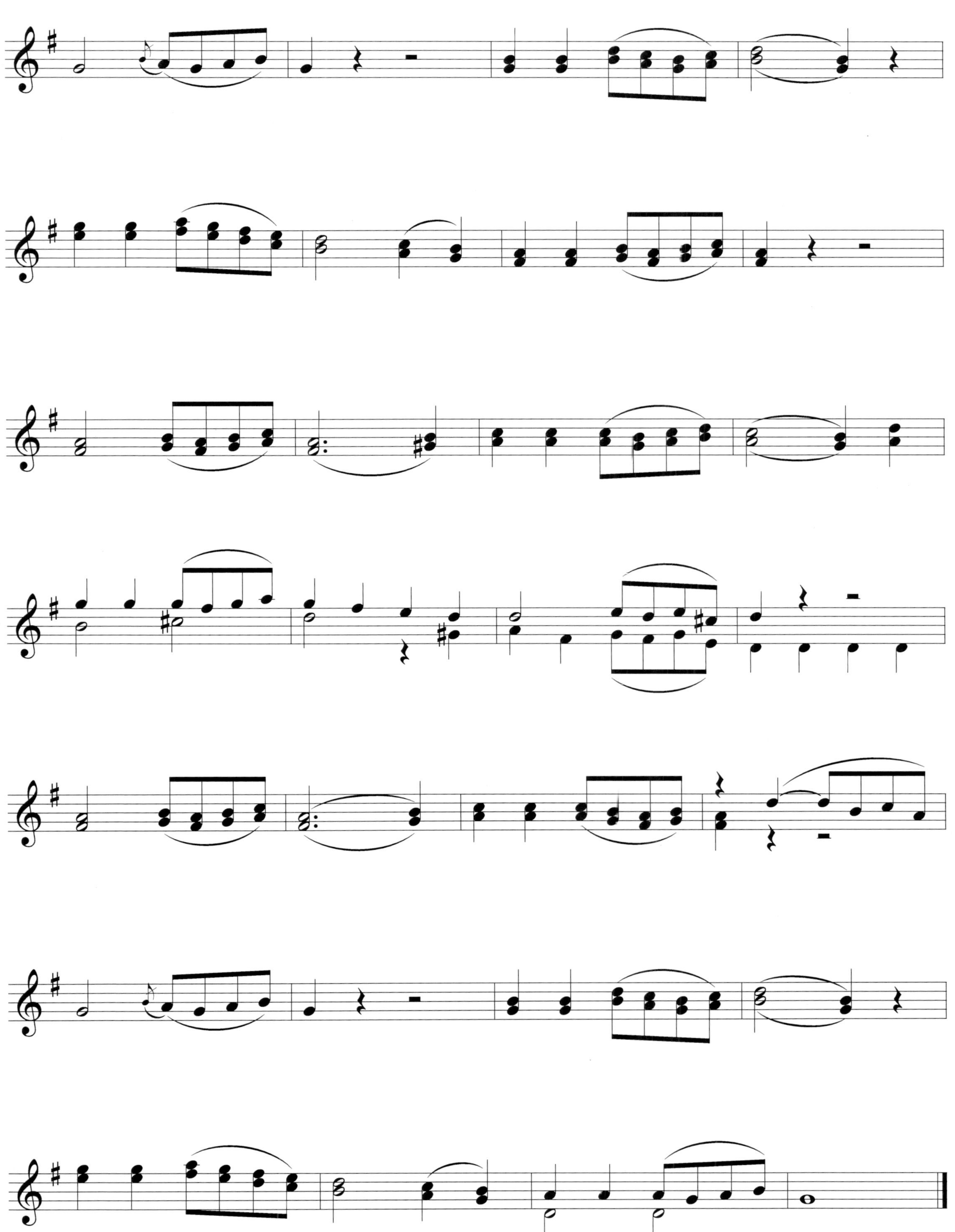

Other Recommended Recorder Books

400 Years of Recorder Music (Weiss)

Baroque Recorder Music (Zeidler)

Classical Repertoire for Recorder (Puscoiu)

Easy Duets for Soprano Recorder (Puscoiu)

Famous Melodies for Recorder (Weiss)

Medieval and Renaissance Music for Recorder (Bancalari)

Recorder in the Baroque Era (Bancalari)

Solo Pieces for the Beginning Descant/Soprano Recorder (Puscoiu)

Solo Pieces for the Intermediate Descant/Soprano Recorder (Puscoiu)

Solo Pieces for the Advanced Descant/Soprano Recorder (Puscoiu)

Celtic Tunes for Recorder (Diehl)

Folklore of the World (Paulsen-Bahnsen)

Early American Roots: Recorder Edition (Wysham/Reiss)

Folk Melodies for Recorder (Weiss)

Native American Music for Recorder (Constas)

Recorder Solos on Balkan Folk Songs and Dances (Puscoiu)

The Complete Scottish & English Country Dance Master for Recorders (O'Scannell)

Solos for Soprano Recorder Collection 6: British Melodies (Kimberling)

Solos for Soprano Recorder Collection 7: Melodies by Women Composers (Kimberling)

Solos for Soprano Recorder Collection 8: Eastern European & Jewish Melodies (Kimberling)

Chants and Reflections for Recorder (Constas)

Christmas Carols for Recorder (Zeidler)

Hymns & Sacred Melodies for Recorder (W. Bay)

Wedding Music for Recorder (Constas)

WWW.MELBAY.COM